CROSS-COUNTRY SKI TOURS

WASHINGTON'S
North Cascades

SECOND EDITION

CROSS-COUNTRY SKI TOURS

WASHINGTON'S
North Cascades
SECOND EDITION

Tom Kirkendall & Vicky Spring

THE
MOUNTAINEERS

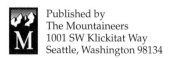

Published by
The Mountaineers
1001 SW Klickitat Way
Seattle, Washington 98134

0 9 8 7 6
5 4 3 2 1

Published simultaneously in Canada by Douglas & McIntyre, Ltd., 1615 Venables Street, Vancouver, B.C. V5L 2H1

Published simultaneously in Great Britain by Cordee, 3a DeMontfort Street, Leicester, England, LE1 7HD

Manufactured in Canada

Edited by Dana Fos
Maps by Tom Kirkendall
All photographs by Kirkendall/Spring Photographers
Cover and book design by The Mountaineers Books
Book layout by Gray Mouse Graphics

Cover photograph: *Skier at Echo Ridge cross-country area near Chelan (Tour 60)*
Frontispiece: *Old warming hut overlooking Bagley Lakes (Tour 11)*

Library of Congress Cataloging-in-Publication Data
Kirkendall, Tom.
    Cross-country ski tours : Washington's north Cascades / Tom Kirkendall & Vicky Spring. — 2nd ed.
        p.   cm.
    Rev. ed. of: Cross-country ski tours of Washington's north Cascades. c1988
    Includes bibliographical references (p.   ).
    ISBN 0-89886-483-6
    1. Cross-country skiing—Cascade Range—Guidebooks. 2. Cross-country skiing—Washington (State)—Guidebooks. 3. Cascade Range—Guidebooks. 4. Washington (State)—Guidebooks. I. Spring, Vicky, 1953–   . II. Kirkendall, Tom. Cross-country ski tours of Washington's north Cascades. III. Title.
GV854.5.C27K57   1996
917.97'5—dc20   96–20139
                                                              CIP

See and Ski Trail

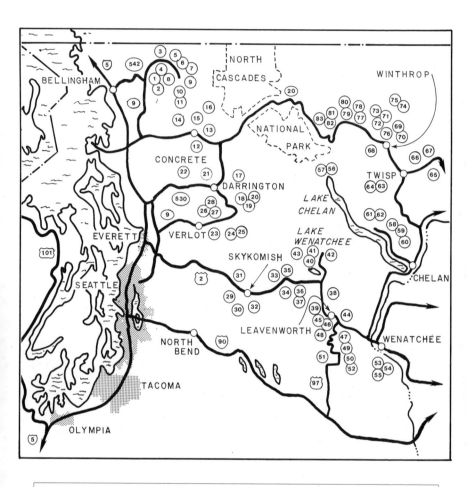

A NOTE ABOUT SAFETY

Safety is an important concern in all outdoor activities. No guidebook can alert you to every hazard or anticipate the limitations of every reader. Therefore, the descriptions of roads, trails, routes, and natural features in this book are not representations that a particular place or excursion will be safe for your party. When you follow any of the routes described in this book, you assume responsibility for your own safety. Under normal conditions, such excursions require the usual attention to traffic, road and trail conditions, weather, terrain, the capabilities of your party, and other factors. Keeping informed on current conditions and exercising common sense are the keys to a safe, enjoyable outing.

The Mountaineers

CONTENTS

THE CROSS-COUNTRY SKIERS' SCOREBOARD

In the rosy glow of the 1980s, it seemed that the overcutting of timber on forest lands was, if anything, a boon to the cross-country skier: more forest roads to explore in the winter, more clearcuts for downhill runs, and easier access to high meadows. Now it is the 1990s and reality has set in. The Forest Service is out of funds and essentially closing down. You might not think that the budget woes of the Forest Service will have an effect on the average cross-country skier—but they do.

Already we are seeing the effects of the new economy. Nonessential roads are being trenched and abandoned. Where touring was good just five years ago, vegetation is closing in, leaving roads all but impassable. The saddest losses are the short roads: Red Bridge Tour up Gordon Ridge and the skier-only Double Eagle Road in the popular Verlot winter recreation area.

All the news is not bad. The growth of volunteerism is raising cheers deep in the district offices of the Forest Service and hope in the hearts of all outdoor users. Anderson Creek and Razor Hone Roads are a sterling example of what can be done with time, effort, and determination. Both roads were nearly lost under a wall of brush when a volunteer group out of Bellingham organized and saved them. Using Sno-Park funds and a lot of back-breaking work they ensured that skiers had guaranteed parking and open roads to ski on, and then they went one step further and added grooming.

The Bellingham group serves as a good example for all skiers. Roads can be kept open, if we are willing to put in the time and effort to do it.

Once again, it must be stressed that our winter recreation does not come with a guarantee. The revenues and funds no longer exist for land managers to maintain the same services they have in the past. Skiers must rely on their own efforts if they wish to ensure the same quality of excellence they are accustomed to. If you would like to become involved in keeping a few roads from becoming overgrown, form a plan then take it to a local Forest Service Office for approval. Reviving roads after they have nearly drowned in brush is a fearsome task. Generally this activity requires a group effort, so get together with some friends and have a great time preserving our winter wonderland.

As no local publication exists that deals exclusively with skiers' activities, we find *Pack and Paddle Magazine* to be the best means available for passing information, sharing concerns, initiating letter-writing campaigns, looking for fellow volunteers, and communicating with other skiers. Subscriptions can be obtained by writing to Pack and Paddle, P.O. Box 1063, Port Orchard, WA 98366.

Opposite: *Skiing a groomed trail along the shore of Lake Wenatchee. Dirtyface Peak is in the distance.*

11

Kick-turn

Guaranteeing our winter wonderland will not be a quick or an easy process. But if the Forest Service and the Parks Department know that we skiers are concerned with protecting and expanding our access into the forests and that any action depriving us of this very limited resource will be answered by a flood of protest, we will have gone a long way toward writing our own guarantee.

MAPS NOT INTENDED FOR NAVIGATION	
(90) INTERSTATE FREEWAYS	(34) SKI TOUR NUMBER
(2) U.S. HIGHWAYS	AVALANCHE HAZARD
(20) STATE HIGHWAYS	⌂ LODGE
[69] MAINLINE FOREST ROADS	⊔ HUT
[137] SPUR FOREST ROADS	
DRIVING ROADS	SKIING ROADS
SKI LIFT	SKIING TRAILS

INTRODUCTION

Washington's Cascade Mountains provide infinite opportunity for excellent cross-country skiing whether on groomed trails, scenic logging roads, or open slopes of dormant volcanoes. This book is just an introduction to the vast amount of skiing that can be found. Particular emphasis has been given to the needs of the beginning and intermediate skier, but trails and routes have been included that will test the backcountry skier and challenge the mountaineer.

To repeat the caution that any guidebook must offer, conditions are constantly changing. The reader must always keep the publication date of this book in mind. If you ski onto the scene a couple of years later, you must understand that the authors have no control over (1) the building of new roads or the loss of old ones, (2) new rules and budget constrictions of government agencies, (3) the falling down of trees and the piling up (or not piling up) of snow, (4) the closure of old Sno-Parks and the opening of new ones, and (5) the location of groomed trails at commercial cross-country ski resorts. In a word: Conditions are never the same twice, so be flexible in your plans. However, all budget considerations aside, the largest variable is the snow itself. The Cascade Mountains lie in a maritime climate and the temperatures and amount of snowfall fluctuate wildly from year to year. Never take the snow for granted!!!

HEADING OUT INTO WINTER

This book doesn't explain *how* to ski, just *where*. However, some tips are offered to help orient skiers toward wintertime fun. Further information can be found in Suggested Reading.

BE FLEXIBLE

During research for this book, many Ranger Districts and ski patrols were interviewed and one point was stressed: Be flexible. Have an alternate, safer trip planned if weather changes to create a high avalanche potential in your favorite area. If your second choice is also unsafe, then make your third choice a walk along a beach or to the city park. Your exercise of good judgment will help Ranger Districts and ski areas avoid the necessity of total winter closure for *all* users in order to protect a few thoughtless ones from their own stupidity.

SNO-PARKS

Many of the tours in this book start from Sno-Parks. These are designated parking areas, set aside throughout the winter for recreation. Permits are required to park in these areas and the fees are for plowing, outhouses, signs, and in some areas grooming. Cars parked without permits can count on an expensive ticket and possible towing. Sno-Park permits are sold by the day, weekend, or season. Before you head out, check the Access section of your chosen tour to determine whether or not you will need a permit.

Sno-Park permits are available at many outdoor equipment retail stores or by mail from: Office of Winter Recreation, Washington State Parks and Recreation Commission, 7150 Cleanwater Lane KY-11, P.O. Box 42650, Olympia, WA 98504-2650.

HUTS

As veterans of many long winter nights in a small mountain tent we understand the appeal of a comfortable warm hut. Unfortunately, very few huts are available to skiers. In the northern half of the Cascades Mountains

A happy hut skier

huts are found in two areas. The Rendevous Hut system in the Methow Valley consists of six huts, five of which are interconnected on a system of groomed trails. The sixth hut is located, intriguingly, in the backcountry. The huts are operated by Rendezvous Outfitters, Inc. of Winthrop. For information call 1-800-422-3048. Gear hauling services are also available. (See Tours 71, 73, and 77 for more information.) The Scottish Lakes in the Chiwaukum Mountains have seven cabins for overnighting at the edge of the Alpine Lakes Wilderness. Gear- and people-hauling services are available. For more information contact High Country Adventures, Inc., P.O. Box 2023, Snohomish, WA 98291-2023. Or call (206) 844-2000. (See Tour 37 for more information.)

WINTER CAMPING

For the hearty and independent-minded, winter camping is a fun way to go. Unlike summer camping, reservations are not required and very few restrictions are placed on where you can set up your tent in the backcountry. However, there is a whole realm of special challenges that the winter camper must face: finding a safe site, building a solid tent platform, staying warm, keeping happily occupied on nights that last from 4 P.M. to 8 A.M., finding water or melting snow, and proper disposal of human waste. The amount of gear needed for a successful trip is a bit staggering. If you are unsure of how to deal with these issues, take an experienced winter camper with you on your first trip.

Always carry out your garbage. (If you packed it in full, you can pack it out empty.) When spending the day or several days out skiing, take care where you park your car. A sudden winter storm can cover bare and dry logging roads and make driving back out impossible until spring. Always travel with a shovel and keep a watchful eye on the weather.

Campgrounds: Most Forest Service campgrounds are locked and gated by mid-September. Only two campgrounds were still open throughout the winter as of 1995. One is located on the Mountain Loop Highway beyond Verlot. The other is the south section of Lake Wenatchee State Park. Lake Wenatchee State Park offers a three-sided shelter for cooking as well as the luxuries of running water and a heated restroom.

Other Camp Areas: Unless otherwise posted, Sno-Parks make excellent impromptu camping areas. You may park and sleep in a van or car or pitch your tent on a nearby snow bank. (If you pitch your tent in the parking lot you may spend an hour or more in the middle of the night wondering if the snowplow is going to run you over.)

STEHEKIN

Located at the upper end of Lake Chelan, the only winter access to Stehekin is by boat or float plane. Most visitors take advantage of the relatively inexpensive boat service. In the winter the *Lady Express* runs 5 days a week. You may board the boat in Chelan or save a little money and pick it up at Fields Landing. Once in Stehekin, accommodations range from hotel rooms or cabins at the Stehekin Lodge to bed and breakfast facilities. Of course you may camp; the North Cascades National Park leaves the campground near the boat dock open all winter. If camping, bring a shovel to level a tent platform on the hard snow under the trees. Water is available at the park offices located above the post office.

Once in Stehekin you must still go up-valley a minimum of 3 miles to reach the first cross-country ski trails. In 1995, winter transportation was being handled by the Stehekin Lodge. Stop in at the store when you arrive to arrange your schedule.

Although most of the tourist facilities at Stehekin shut down during the winter, the store and restaurant at the Stehekin Lodge are open throughout the winter. Snowshoe and ski rentals are available.

For information concerning rates and schedules of the *Lady Express* contact the Lake Chelan Boat Company at (509) 682-4584. For reservations and information concerning the Stehekin Lodge and transportation to the ski trails call (509) 682-4494.

WHAT TO TAKE

Every skier who ventures more than a few feet away from the car should be prepared to spend the night out. Winter storms can come with great speed and force, creating whiteouts that leave the skier with nowhere to go. Each ski pack must include the Ten Essentials, plus one:

1. Extra clothing—more than needed in the worst of weather. (See More Words Concerning Clothing, below.)
2. Extra food and water—there should be some left over at the end of the trip.
3. Sunglasses—a few hours of bright sun on snow can cause a pounding headache or temporary blindness.
4. Knife—for first aid and emergency repairs.
5. First-aid kit—just in case.
6. Fire starter—chemical starter to get wet wood burning.
7. Waterproof matches in a waterproof container with a striker that you have tested before you leave home—to start a fire.
8. Flashlight—be sure to have extra batteries as well as an extra bulb.
9. Map—make sure it's the right one for the trip.
10. Compass—keep in mind the declination.

Plus: Repair kit—including a spare ski tip, spare screws and binding bail (if changeable), heavy-duty tape, and a combination wrench–pliers–screwdriver.

Other handy items to carry include a small shovel, sun cream, and a large plastic tarp to use as a "picnic blanket" or as an emergency shelter. All these items should fit comfortably into a day pack. (Obviously, a fanny pack is

Winter campsite on Schweitzer Creek Loop (Tour 24)

too small. Fanny packs are strictly for track and resort skiing where one is carrying only a sandwich and a few waxes.)

MORE WORDS CONCERNING CLOTHING

There is no dress code for cross-country skiing. Clothing can be anything from high-fashion lycra to mismatched army surplus. However, most of the garments sold as cross-country ski clothing are designed for resort skiing or racing, providing flexibility and style, but not much warmth.

In the wilderness, warmth is crucial. Cover your body from head to toe in synthetic long underwear, or wool if you like to itch. Next add two or more layers on the upper body, such as a synthetic shirt and a pile sweater. The lower body should get at least one more layer such as a pair of lightly insulated pants. Top it all off with some raingear of coated nylon or breathable waterproof material. Be prepared to strip down to the inmost layers on warm days.

SKIS AND BOOTS

What length of ski to buy, with side-cut or without, with metal edges or without, hard or soft camber? What boots are best, flexible or stiff? These and many more questions could fill a book—and they do. Our one and only suggestion is to purchase a waxless ski as your first pair. Learning to ski can be complicated enough without the frustration of trying to wax for the ever-changing snow conditions of the Cascade Mountains. When looking for that new pair of skis, avoid stores that just happen to have a few cross-country skis in stock. Stores that have special cross-country departments and employees who enjoy cross-country skiing in the Cascades or Olympic Mountains will be able to give you a better understanding of what you need.

Cross-country boots come in two varieties, lightweight for track skiing and touring, and heavyweight for backcountry and telemark skiing. The type of boots you have will determine the type of bindings you need, so buy the boots first.

TECHNIQUE

Cross-country skiing looks simple enough, but proper technique is very important to ensure a good time. Even expert downhillers have problems the first day on cross-country skis. The narrow skis, flexibility of the bindings, and softness of the shoes give an entirely different feeling. Books are helpful, but one or two lessons may be needed. Many organizations offer a two-lesson plan, the first to get you started in the right direction and the second to correct any problems you have.

PETS

Although in some jurisdictions the family pet is permitted to tag along on summer hikes, wintertime should be left to the two-legged family members. Skiing through knee-deep powder is lots of fun, but not for the ski-less family pet, floundering in a white morass. Pets also tend to destroy ski tracks by leaving behind deep paw prints and brown klister.

Pets are not allowed in National Parks or on any groomed ski trails.

FURTHER INFORMATION

The following is a list of phone numbers that may be helpful when planning your winter trips.

Groomed Area Snow Conditions

Echo Valley Cross Country 1-800-4-CHELAN
Lake Wenatchee State Park (509) 763-3103
Leavenworth Winter Sports Club (509) 548-5115
Methow Valley Ski Touring Association 1-800-682-5787

Forest Service

Chelan Ranger Station (509) 682-2576
Darrington Ranger Station (360) 436-1155

Leavenworth Ranger Station (509) 548-5817 or 780-1413
Mount Baker Ranger District (360) 856-5700
North Cascades National Park (360) 856-5700
Skykomish Ranger Station (360) 677-2414
Twisp Ranger Station (509) 997-2131
Verlot Public Service Center (360) 691-7791
Winthrop Ranger Station (509) 996-2266

GUIDE TO THE GUIDEBOOK

The following is an explanation of how to best make use of the information in this book and what some of the commonly employed terms mean in non-skier English.

TYPES OF TOURS

At the head of each route description is a short synopsis of pertinent information. When you are ready to select a tour you need only scan this information to determine if you wish to read the entire description. The following is an explanation of terms.

Class: Short for classification, this entry classifies each trail by usage:

Groomed: These are skier-only trails that have been smoothed out by a machine to provide the best possible skiing conditions. As grooming is expensive and time-consuming, a fee is often charged to ski in these areas. Dogs are not allowed on groomed trails.

You will find several types of grooming; the simplest is snow compacted by a snowmobile or snow cat on a regular basis. Some trails are *groomed and tracked* by a machine that compacts the snow then leaves grooves for skis. Finally, *groomed for skating* means there is a lane, wide enough for the sweeping stride of a skater on standard-length skate skis.

Groomed trails provide stability and aid with ski management, something beginners and two- to five-year-old skiers appreciate very much.

Self-Propelled: These are areas closed to snowmobiles or other mechanical forms of transport. These trails are not groomed nor are they designated as skier-only. You may have the company of snowshoers and hikers on a self-propelled tour.

Multiple Use: These are tours on roads or trails that are open to snowmobiles and possibly even four-wheel-drive trucks.

Rating: Each tour has been rated for difficulty based on the amount of skill required to enjoy the trip. The rating is located in the information block at the head of the tour's description. For the sake of simplicity we have used five categories which tend to be broad and somewhat overlapping; consider them to be merely suggestions.

Easiest: No skill requirement. Anyone can have fun the very first time on skis and families will find easiest tours to be great for very small children.

Many of these tours are in areas where sleds loaded with gear or children can be pulled with relative ease. *Easiest* tours generally are on level logging roads or abandoned railroad grades. Many groomed and tracked areas will have trails that are rated *easiest*.

More Difficult: The minimum skills required are good balance, kick and glide, and simple stopping techniques such as pole dragging, snowplowing, and sitting down—as well as a finely developed sense of humor. The tours at this level are generally on logging roads, marked Forest Service loops, or groomed tracks that cover some steep terrain.

Most Difficult: Tours that receive this designation may be long or very steep, or both. Skiers who attempt these tours should have endurance and the ability to descend steep slopes in all types of snow conditions. Minimum required skills include the kick-turn, herringbone, and snowplow turn. Skiers who can telemark will enjoy these tours more than those who cannot. *Most difficult* tours are generally on narrow, steep logging roads and may have optional *backcountry* side trips and descent routes.

Coal Lake Road

Backcountry: The minimum skills required for these tours are full control of skis at all times, mastery of the telemark or any turn, and the ability to stop quickly. Some backcountry tours require basic routefinding skills.

Mountaineer: In addition to *backcountry* skiing skills, *mountaineer* trips require competence in routefinding, knowledge of snow and avalanche conditions, glacier travel techniques, weather savvy, winter camping skills, winter survival skills, and mountaineering skills.

One Way/Round Trip: Snow levels vary from year to year and from day to day. Therefore, the starting point of your tour, especially on logging roads, may vary with the snow. A base point (which may or may not be your actual starting point) has been assigned (in some cases arbitrarily) to each tour. Miles to the trip objective and back again are computed from this point.

Skiing Time: This is the time spent skiing to and from the destination and does *not* include lunch or rest stops. The times are calculated from the route's base point. If the snowline is above this point, less time will be required; if the snow level has dipped lower, more time may be needed to complete the trip. The times given for each trail assume good conditions. If a track must be broken through heavy snow or the surface is extremely hard ice, add a generous amount of extra time.

Elevation Gain: The elevation gain entry helps you determine the amount of climbing you must do between the parking lot, or base point, and your destination. When possible, ups-and-downs have been calculated into the total elevation gain.

High Point: This entry notes the highest point you will reach on your tour. You will find the high point an important piece of information when the snow level is fluctuating wildly or when the winter has been unseasonably warm.

Best: This category makes an attempt to predict the unpredictable by stating when skiing is best for each route. To make these predictions certain generalizations have been made based on a mythical average snow year. The time band given is a narrow one. Skiing often starts as much as a month before given times and lasts a month after. If in doubt, call the area ranger station, listen to pass reports, or contact local mountain shops before starting out.

AVALANCHE POTENTIAL

Tours in this book have been selected for their safety and no known areas of extreme hazard have been included. The warnings given are about areas to avoid at times when the snow is unstable. To know when these times are, you must make it your responsibility to inform yourself about current weather and snow conditions. The best source for up-to-date information on the weather and avalanche conditions in the Washington Cascades and Olympics is a weather radio with continuous reports from the NOAA (National Oceanic and Atmospheric Administration). For specific tours call the ranger station in that district; on weekends there will be a recorded message. If all else fails, talk with knowledgeable experts at your local cross-country ski shop.

Your best defense against avalanches is knowledge. Check Suggested Reading for references. Several things to particularly watch for are as follows:

- Avalanche danger is especially high during warming trends or after a heavy snowfall; at these times avoid leeward slopes and travel on ridge tops.
- Steep hillsides, particularly north-facing, may remain shaded through the winter months. When the sun finally climbs over the hill in March or April, these hills may be covered by spring, or climax, avalanches.
- Wind causes snow to build up on the leeward side of ridges, creating dangerous overhangs called cornices. Often you cannot tell whether or not a ridge has a cornice even when you are on the top. Never ski beyond the line of trees or snowblown rocks that mark the true crest of a ridge unless you have first checked for cornices. It is as dangerous to ski under a cornice as over it. Cornices may break off and trigger avalanches below.

Forecasting agencies express the daily hazard in the following four classifications:

1. Low Avalanche Hazard—mostly stable snow.
2. Moderate Avalanche Hazard—areas of unstable snow on steep, open slopes or gullies.
3. High Avalanche Hazard—snow pack very unstable. Avalanches highly probable on steep slopes and in gullies.
4. Extreme Avalanche Hazard—travel in the mountains unsafe. Time for a Mexican vacation.

These classifications of hazard have to do with the weather's contribution to the avalanches. Each trail in this book has been rated as to the potential of the terrain for avalanches. The two factors, hazard (which changes daily) and potential, must be put together by the skier to make an accurate judgment of the situation.

If the avalanche potential for the trail is listed as *none,* the trail may be safely skied on days when the hazard is low, moderate, or high.

Areas with *low* avalanche potential normally may be skied on days when the hazard is low or moderate.

A *moderate* avalanche potential indicates the area is always to be skied with caution and then only when the hazard is low.

Avalanche forecasting is not an exact science. Skiers must accept a certain amount of risk when skiing outside of patrolled areas. Use the forecast only as a guide; pockets of unstable snow may exist in areas that have been predicted to be safe. Always seek up-to-date avalanche information before each trip, even for trips of *low* to *moderate* avalanche potential. And always rely on your own best judgment, even if no hazards are forecasted.

MAPS

Blankets of snow add new difficulties to routefinding. Signs are covered, road junctions are obscured, and trails blend into the surrounding countryside. Always carry a good map of the area where you will be skiing.

To help you find the best map for your tour, we have recommended a topographic map (USGS, Green Trails, USFS, or MVSTA) in each tour description. The USGS maps are published by the U.S. Geological Survey. These 7½-minute maps cover the entire country and are unequaled for off-road and off-trail routefinding. Unfortunately, USGS maps are not very accurate in terms of road and trail coverage. Green Trails are 15-minute maps published in Washington that show some of the more popular skiing and snowmobile routes. These maps do not cover areas beyond the heartland of the Cascades and Olympics.

The USFS (U.S. Forest Service) Ranger District maps show contours, roads, and trails for an entire ranger district. These outstanding maps are on a 15-minute base and sold at a bargain price. They are the most up-to-date maps available. Handle with care: the maps are huge and tear easily.

Both the USGS and Green Trails maps are available at outdoor equipment stores and many Forest Service Ranger Stations. The USFS Ranger District maps are mainly available through the Forest Service and may be purchased in person or by mail-order from the Ranger District Offices or from the Forest Headquarters office.

The MVSTA (Methow Valley Ski Touring Association) maps recommended for some tours in the Methow Valley are shaded relief rather than topographic. They give a feeling for the terrain but do not show exact elevation. These maps are recommended only for tours on groomed trails and are the only maps that correctly depict all the intersections. MVSTA maps are supplied free-of-charge when you buy a trail pass.

Another excellent resource is an up-to-date Forest Service Recreation Map, available for a small fee at Ranger Stations (on weekdays) or by writing the district offices.

1 GLACIER CREEK

Lookout Mountain

Class: multiple use
Rating: easiest
Round trip: 11 miles
Skiing time: 5 hours
Elevation gain: 2,000 feet
High point: 4,780 feet
Best: December and March–mid-April
Avalanche potential: low
Map: Green Trails, Mt. Baker No. 13

Mount Baker Vista

Class: multiple use
Rating: more difficult
Round trip: 8 miles
Skiing time: 4 hours
Elevation gain: 2,500 feet
High point: 5,200 feet
Best: December and March–mid-April
Avalanche potential: moderate
Map: Green Trails, Mt. Baker No. 13

Early and late season are the best times to enjoy the unbeatable views and easy terrain of the Glacier Creek area. Two destinations are recommended here. Both are extremely scenic and both offer opportunities to leave the roads and head into the backcountry.

Expect to encounter snowmobiles on Glacier Creek Road all winter long. Early and late in the season the numbers are not overwhelming, but by midwinter the going gets ugly. For optimum enjoyment of this tour, avoiding both the snowmobiles and a long slog up-valley, ski here when the road is open to around the 2,000-foot level.

Access: Drive Mount Baker Highway 542, to the town of Glacier. Continue 0.6 mile beyond the Forest Service Information Center then turn right on Glacier Creek Road No. 39. Head up the valley on the narrow, paved road until blocked by snow. When conditions are best, the road should be open between Coal Creek at the 5-mile mark and Lookout Creek near the 6-mile mark.

Icicle

Lookout Mountain: Glacier Creek Road climbs steadily through second-growth forest with few views until clearcuts are reached 2 miles above Coal Creek. At 2½ miles the road divides (3,500 feet). Before turning right on Road 36, feast your eyes on the towering walls of Chowder Ridge, the rounded dome of Hadley Peak, Roosevelt and Coleman Glaciers, and the dark profile of the Black Buttes looming over Heliotrope and Grouse Ridges.

For the next 2 miles, Road 36 heads into the Lookout Creek drainage, climbing gently. After crossing Lookout Creek at 4½ miles, reach an intersection (4, 100 feet). Options abound. For the best views stay right and continue on Road 3610 and head towards the top of Lookout Mountain. Road 3610 ends a mile later just below the lower summit of Lookout Mountain (4,780 feet).

Mount Baker Vista: From the Road 36 turnoff, 2½ miles above Coal Creek, continue straight ahead on Road 39. The road reaches the Mount

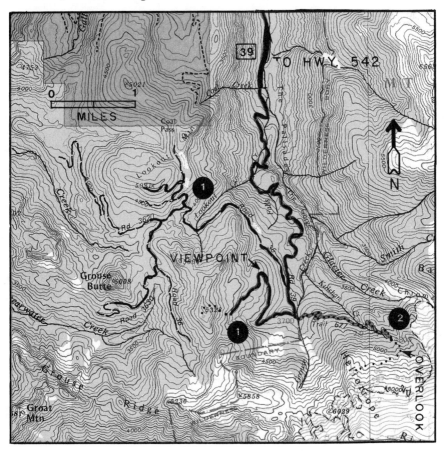

Baker Vista, a viewpoint worthy of a long rest at 4,200 feet, 4 miles from Coal Creek.

If time and energy allow, continue up the road to its end at 4,500 feet and then ski west to the summit of a 5,328-foot hill. The snowmobiles head to the open meadows here, and skiers who hide their pride can follow the machine tracks to excellent snow on the flanks of Grouse Ridge. Exercise caution: steeper hillsides can slide after a heavy snowfall or on warmer spring days.

Winter forest scene

2 HELIOTROPE RIDGE

Class: self-propelled
Rating: backcountry
Round trip: 13 miles to
    Coleman Glacier viewpoint
Skiing time: 1–2 days
Elevation gain: 3,700 feet

High point: 6,500 feet
Best: November and March–May
Avalanche potential: low
Map: Green Trails, Mt. Baker No. 13

See map on page 25

From a camp near the edge of crevasse-slashed Coleman Glacier, carve ski tracks across miles of untracked slopes on Heliotrope Ridge. In the evening return to the doorstep of the tent and watch one of nature's best shows, as a brief, brilliant winter sunset casts pinks and golds over the snowy ramparts of Mount Baker— or maybe crawl in the tent and peer out at a blizzard.

The route to the northwest side of Mount Baker culminates in 3 miles of trail but starts with 10 miles of road, some or all of which may have to be skied. Because the road is extremely popular with motorized sled riders, human-powered travelers are advised to do this trip in fall or spring when the road is partially or totally snow- and noise-free. A special warning about late fall: If you are not careful, your car could be snowed in for the winter. If 6 inches of snow piles up at your camp in the mountains, it is time to leave—or already be gone.

Access: Drive Highway 542 to Glacier and register your trip at the Forest Service Information Center on the east end of town. At 0.6 mile past the Information Center turn right on Glacier Creek Road and follow it to the snowline or trailhead.

Skier on Heliotrope Ridge

At 5 miles the road bumps over Coal Creek and starts serious climbing. This generally marks the beginning of spring skiing (2,000 feet).

The Tour: Occasional views of Coleman Glacier and its headwall on the glacier-tracked face of Mount Baker enliven the initial miles up the steadily climbing road. At a large junction at 2½ miles stay left on Road 39 for the final ¼ mile to the trailhead parking lot (3,700 feet).

To find the trail, descend into the heavy timber at the east side of the parking area. The trail is somewhat discernible all winter. Cross a small creek then begin climbing. Skiers with skins will probably wish to use them. Many find it preferable to walk.

Two miles up the trail (4,700 feet), reach the site of Kulshan Cabin, torn down in 1986. Pass several campsites here. Unless the weather is foul,

Mount Baker's Coleman Glacier Overlook

continue on to scenic sites beyond. Before long the trail will divide; continue straight ahead. One mile beyond the old cabin site the trail ends at the Coleman Glacier Overlook. Small campsites may be found 500 feet west of the Overlook in a band of scraggly trees.

The best skiing lies west of the Overlook, separated from it by a series of steep, slide-prone gullies. Ski up open slopes from the Overlook, bearing right. Reach a broad bench at about 6,500 feet then bear right. Ski west over rolling Heliotrope Ridge and try out some of the steep slopes and bowls beyond.

Many skiers find the long open slopes leading to the summit of Mount Baker extremely alluring. However, the attempt must not be made without climbing gear as deep crevasses lie hidden under the smooth snow.

3 CANYON CREEK

Class: multiple use
Rating: most difficult
Round trip: 4–10 miles
Skiing time: 2–6 hours
Elevation gain: up to 3,000 feet

High point: 5,699 feet on Excelsior Peak
Best: mid-March–May
Avalanche potential: low
Map: Green Trails, Mt. Baker No. 13

Throughout the winter Canyon Creek Road and its many offshoots are a popular haunt of snowmobilers. However, when the spring sun starts shining and the noisy snow machines are set aside for noisier jet skis, skiers are free to explore the scenic Canyon Creek drainage in peace.

Note: This road suffers from frequent washouts. Be flexible or check ahead with the Mount Baker Forest District Office in Sedro Woolley.

Access: Drive Highway 542 east to Glacier and on for 2 more miles. Turn left on Canyon Creek Road No. 31 and go to your choice of the options below.

Kidney Creek Road: At the 7.5-mile point of Road 31, turn right on Road 3130 (2,150 feet), and drive to the snowline. Kidney Creek Road climbs steadily up a steep hillside, through clearcuts and forest, to an intersection at 6½ miles (4,900 feet). The left fork (Road 3130) continues north ½ mile along the ridge top to views of Canyon Creek, Bald Mountain, and the Coast Range of British Columbia. The right fork (Spur 017) follows the ridge south for another mile. Backcountry skiers may continue on beyond the road-end (at 5,500 feet) to open meadows below Church Mountain.

Whistler Creek Road: Ten miles up Canyon Creek Road No. 31 take a right onto Road 3160 (2,600 feet). Cross Canyon Creek and follow Whistler Creek 1½ miles before starting a seriously steep climb. At 4 miles from the intersection the road arrives at the top of the ridge and ends (4,700 feet).

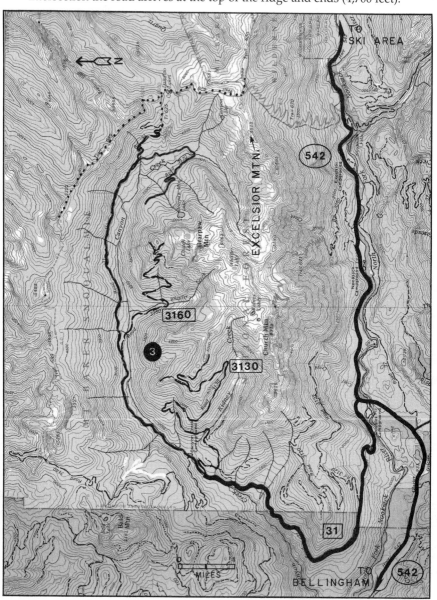

Excelsior Mountain Trail (recommended for backcountry or mountaineer skiers): For the greatest of late, late spring skiing as well as spectacular views, drive Road 31 for 15 miles from Highway 542 to the Excelsior Mountain Trailhead (4,200 feet). The trail climbs through timber, gaining 300 feet in the first ½ mile to meet the Canyon Ridge Trail. Go right, passing to the east of the Damfino Lakes (4,500 feet). Ski the next mile up through forest, then climb a gully to reach meadows at 5,100 feet, 2½ miles from the road. To the south is a spectacular view of Baker and Shuksan. To the north are the white-topped Border Peaks and the glacier-coated Coast Range. Plan to spend at least one entire day telemarking on the long, rolling snow-covered meadows.

Shoulder of Church Mountain from Kidney Creek Road

Mount Sefrit from the overlook

4 WELLS CREEK

Winter Viewpoint

Class: *multiple use*
Rating: *most difficult*
Round trip: *6 miles*
Skiing time: *4 hours*
Elevation gain: *1,100 feet*
High point: *2,600 feet*
Best: *mid-December–February*
Avalanche potential: *none*
Map: *Green Trails, Mt. Baker No. 13*

Cougar Divide

Class: *multiple use*
Rating: *backcountry*
Round trip: *up to 16 miles*
Skiing time: *1–2 days*
Elevation gain: *2,400 feet*
High point: *4,900 feet*
Best: *April–May*
Avalanche potential: *high in midwinter*
Map: *Green Trails, Mt. Baker No. 13*

An overlook of the Nooksack River valley with views spanning from Church Mountain to the glaciered peaks of Mount Sefrit and Ruth Mountain is the object of the winter tour. In spring, when the snow melts enough

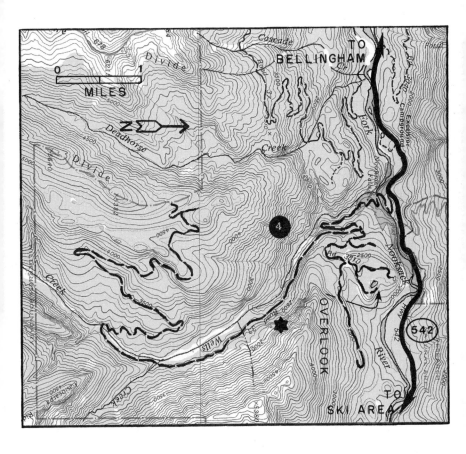

to allow vehicle access partway up the road, the destination becomes the extremely scenic Cougar Divide, which may be followed all the way to the base of Hadley Glacier.

Access: Drive Highway 542 east 6.8 miles beyond the Forest Service Information Center in Glacier. A small parking area usually is plowed at the Wells Creek turnoff (1,700 feet).

Winter Viewpoint: The winter trip starts with a ½-mile descent to the Nooksack River (1,500 feet). The road crosses the river just above Nooksack Falls then climbs slowly but steadily through winter-stilled forest. Just past the 2-mile marker the road forks (2,000 feet). Go left on Road 3310 and stick with it for a steady climb. Pass through young timber plantations until the road splits again at 2¾ miles. Head up and to the left for a steep climb to the crest of a flat-topped knoll. Roam the whole knoll for views from each direction. Take care to stay well back from the edges if not equipped with a parachute—there are cliffs with overhangs and cornices to the north, west, and south.

Cougar Divide: For the spring trip drive, hopefully for several miles, up Wells Creek Road to the snowline. Be sure conditions have stabilized before setting out; open slopes below Barometer Mountain between the 3- and 5-mile markers have a high avalanche potential after a heavy snow. At 5 miles the road leaves Wells Creek and follows Bar Creek for a mile before beginning a long climb towards Cougar Divide. The road splits at the ridge top. The right fork climbs north ½ mile to an overlook of Wells Creek, 5,770-foot Barometer Mountain, and Mount Baker. The left fork heads south ½ mile along the divide. You then may continue backcountry along the rolling ridge crest toward the awesomely glaciered mass of Mount Baker for 2 more miles.

HIGHWAY 542—MOUNT BAKER

5 TWIN LAKES ROAD

Class: multiple use
Rating: more difficult
Round trip: 8 miles
Skiing time: 4 hours
Elevation gain: 1,900 feet

High point: 3,900 feet
Best: mid-December–March
Avalanche potential: low
Map: Green Trails, Mt. Shuksan No. 14

Although it is too dangerous to ski all the way to Twin Lakes, the "safe" section of the road makes an excellent winter tour. The trip back down the steep road is exciting, equally suited for bobsleds as for skis.

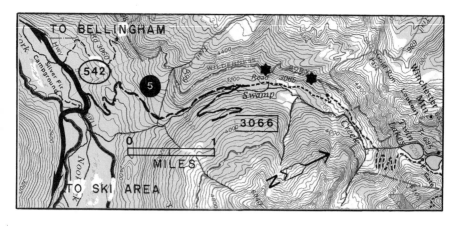

Twin Lakes Road

Access: Drive Mount Baker Highway 542 east 12.5 miles from Glacier. Pass the Department of Highways work sheds and the Twin Lakes Road turnoff and continue on 0.2 mile before turning left at Hannegan Road (Tour 6). Park here (2,200 feet).

The Tour: Walk back along the Mount Baker Highway 0.2 mile to Twin Lakes Road and ski up the hillside through a dense forest of moss-draped trees. At the end of the first mile you will pass a small bench offering a brief respite before the climb resumes with renewed vigor, on the part of the road at least. Pass several spur roads.

Beyond the Keep Kool Trailhead, passed shortly after the 2-mile marker, enter a narrow valley boxed in by Yellow Aster Butte to the west and Goat Mountain to the east. Here the road levels, traversing open slopes above Swamp Creek for nearly ½ mile. Just when the road is set to plunge back into forest is an important junction. This time, take the right fork, Road 3066.

Road 3066 descends briefly to cross Swamp Creek (3,100 feet) then switchbacks up to views of Yellow Aster Butte. After a lazy 1½ miles the road ends at (3,600 feet). Enjoy your flying descent.

 # 6 NORTH FORK NOOKSACK

Class: self-propelled
Rating: easiest
Round trip: 5 miles
Skiing time: 2 hours
Elevation gain: 400 feet

High point: 2,600 feet
Best: January–mid-March
Avalanche potential: low
Map: Green Trails, Mt. Shuksan No. 14

It is unclear whether it is the nearly level terrain, the outstanding scenery, or the closure to snowmobiles that makes this such a popular area. Whatever the reason, the North Fork Nooksack River Road draws novices and experts alike. (Snowmobilers have developed routes around the barriers, so do not expect your tour to be machine-free.)

Access: Drive Highway 542 east from Glacier 12.5 miles. Just before the highway crosses the North Fork Nooksack River, go left on Hannegan Road. Park in the small space provided (2,200 feet).

The Tour: Hannegan Road follows the North Fork Nooksack River upstream along the valley floor, open and level. Views start immediately, Mount Shuksan gleaming in winter white, Mount Sefrit and Ruth Mountain standing out along Nooksack Ridge.

Mount Shuksan towering over the North Fork Nooksack River

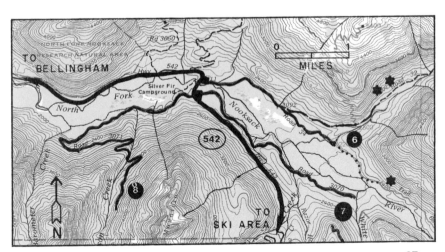

At ½ mile enter the forest. Several spur roads branch off in this area; stay left at all junctions. At 1½ miles the road splits. Hannegan Road No. 32 goes left up Ruth Creek 4 miles to the road-end at Hannegan Campground. Avalanche hazard is high after the first mile and winter travel is not recommended. From the split, North Fork Nooksack River Road No. 34 goes right, skirting the north side of the valley. Road's end is reached in a long mile at the washed-out Ruth Creek bridge.

 # RAZOR HONE ROAD

Class: groomed
Rating: easiest to most difficult
Round trip: 8 miles
Skiing time: 4 hours
Elevation gain: 240 feet

High point: 2,240 feet
Best: mid-December–February
Avalanche potential: low
Map: Green Trails, Mt. Shuksan No. 14

See map on page 37

In this rugged section of the North Cascades the hills sweep up from the river bottoms to the glaciated summits in a near-vertical fashion. The perpendicular nature of the terrain leaves very little room for rambling ski tours. However, with a lot of determination and hours of back-breaking work, the Nooksack Nordic Ski Club has created a groomed ski-touring area. Even beginners and young children can have a good time here. Skaters will find a wide lane just for them and backcountry-equipped skiers can take on the challenge of several steep, abandoned logging roads.

To its credit, this area has the only groomed trails on the west side of the Cascades, north of Stevens Pass. However, the most remarkable feature of this remarkable area is the absence of a trail-use fee.

Despite all the effort to open and groom trails, the weather is capricious. Elevation here is moderate and quality and quantity of the snow vary radically throughout the winter. Do not be surprised if you arrive in midwinter to find little or no snow. Unless you know that the snow has been falling at low elevations, always come with an alternate plan in mind.

Access: Drive Highway 542 east from Glacier 12.8 miles. Five hundred feet after crossing the North Fork Nooksack River, turn left into the large Salmon Ridge Sno-Park (2,200 feet).

The Tour: Razor Hone Road No. 3070 starts at the far end of the open clearing. The groomed road heads east towards the Nooksack River for a

Road-end at the edge of North Fork Nooksack River

few hundred feet before turning southeast to follow the river up-valley. Several trails branch off on either side. Trails on the right loop through the rain forest. To the left, trails head through the brush to the edge of the river.

Razor Hone Road climbs away from the river at ½ mile and descends back to the valley floor again at 1½ miles to cross a creek. Another climb is followed by yet another descent which leads to a crossing of Bagley Creek. Shortly beyond is a steep hill. At the crest a trail (not groomed) branches off to the right and climbs steeply for ½ mile then abruptly ends. The descent is challenging.

Beyond the intersection the road descends into a basin where it passes a second spur road before, at 4 miles, coming to an end at the edge of the Nooksack River.

8 ANDERSON CREEK

Class: *groomed*
Rating: *easiest to more difficult*
Round trip: *10 miles*
Skiing time: *5 hours*
Elevation gain: *1,200 feet*

High point: *3,400 feet*
Best: *mid-December–February*
Avalanche potential: *low*
Map: *Green Trails, Mt. Shuksan No. 14*

See map on page 37

A tour along Anderson Creek Road has two distinctly different parts. The first part is a gentle descent along the floor of the North Fork Nooksack River valley. The second part is a steady climb to views of the snow-and-ice-reamed summits.

Access: Park at the Salmon Ridge Sno-Park (see Tour 7 for driving directions).

The Tour: To begin the tour, carefully cross to the west side of Highway 542. Two roads start here. Stay to the left on Road 3071. (If you make a mistake you will end up skiing loops around Silver Fir Campground.) The first 2 miles goes quickly as your skis follow the gently descending road. This portion of the tour is often groomed with a skating lane in the center and tracks for stride and gliding on the side. The road crosses Anderson Creek for the first time near Mile Post 1. Just before the 2-mile marker the road begins to climb, and the second phase of the tour begins.

At 2½ miles is an intersection (2,200 feet). Follow the main road to the left and continue the climb. This road receives very little maintenance and grooming is possible only if there was sufficient volunteer labor in the fall to cut back the brush and/ or enough snow to cover it. Look for the occasional view of Yellow Aster Butte and Goat Mountain across the valley. Near mile 4 the scene changes as the road crosses Anderson Creek again (3,000 feet), makes a steep

Ice- and snow-covered fir needles

Anderson Creek Road and North Fork Nooksack River valley

switchback, and enters a hanging valley (the natural sweep of the valley was cut off when the Nooksack Glacier scoured out North Fork valley many millennia ago). To the west, the steep sides of Barometer Mountain offer a formidable barrier while Slate Mountain boxes you in on the east.

Shortly after passing the 5-mile marker, the road ends in a clearcut at the Anderson Creek Trailhead, an abandoned trail that goes on up the valley another mile to nowhere in particular. The descent back to the valley floor is quick, but remember to pace yourself for the final, not quite level, stretch along the North Fork Nooksack River.

9 WHITE SALMON CREEK

Class: *self-propelled*
Rating: *more difficult*
Round trip: *5 miles*
Skiing time: *2 hours*
Elevation gain: *320 feet*

High point: *3,840 feet*
Best: *December–mid-April*
Avalanche potential: *none*
Map: *Green Trails, Mt. Shuksan No. 14*

Four words best describe this tour: fun, easy, scenic, and short. The route follows logging roads and clearcuts to the lower slopes of Shuksan Arm, located on the edge of the Mount Baker Wilderness, and offers a front-seat view of glaciers and cliffs rising directly to the summit of Mount Shuksan. This is also a great place to try out the tent on a winter camping adventure.

Access: Drive Mount Baker Highway 542 east 18.6 miles from the town of Glacier. In the middle of a broad corner, find Forest Road 3075 on the left. A plowed parking area at the turnoff marks the start of the tour (3,412 feet).

Chickadee waiting to share your lunch

The Tour: The road makes a short climb then levels to contour around the ridge. Across the Nooksack River valley, Tomyhoi and Yellow Aster Butte are the first peaks visible. After ¾ mile the road bends south, rounding the ridge. At this point you have several options. You may stay with the main road, enjoying incredible views of Mount Shuksan, while descending a steep old clearcut. Do not let the promise of more views lure you farther down than you intended to go. At 1½ miles reach the second switchback, where the road divides (3,125 feet). To the left a road contours north ½ mile to end at the crest of the ridge. The main road continues through the switchback and continues to descend to the 2,800-foot point where it ends at 2¼ miles from the Mount Baker Highway.

For an alternate tour, leave the road at the ¾-mile point and head

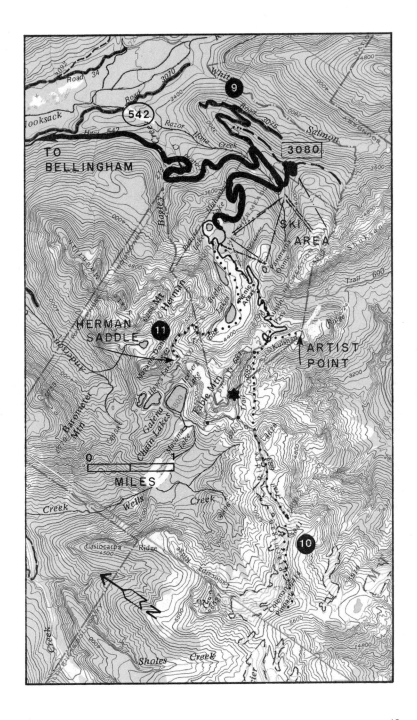

Early winter sunset on Mount Shuksan

cross-country to the right. Ski up through a clearcut then follow the ridge, gaining 150 feet of elevation, to meet Road 3080. Ski up the road ½ mile to the new White Salmon day lodge and parking area for the Mount Baker Ski Area. Either take your skis off and walk around the parking lot or make your way, with your skis on, around the parameter. Ski past the lodge then up the left side of the groomed slopes to find a road heading into the forest. This road is ¾ mile long and ends at the top of a logged clearing, overlooking White Salmon Creek and yielding a front row view of Mount Shuksan. In the spring, thundering avalanches often are seen crashing down the face.

10 ARTIST POINT AND COLEMAN PINNACLE

Artist Point

Class: self-propelled
Rating: backcountry
Round trip: 5 miles
Skiing time: 3 hours
Elevation gain: 1,100 feet
High point: 5,220 feet
Best: December–May
Avalanche potential: low
Map: Green Trails, Mt. Shuksan No. 14

Coleman Pinnacle

Class: self-propelled
Rating: mountaineer
Round trip: 11 miles
Skiing time: 6 hours
Elevation gain: 2,080 feet
High point: 6,200 feet
Best: December–May
Avalanche potential: high
Map: Green Trails, Mt. Shuksan No. 14

See map on page 43

It is not possible to visit Artist Point and come away with any doubts about the source of its name. Located between the vertical massif of Mount Shuksan and the (restlessly?) slumbering dome of Mount Baker you can spend hours contemplating the view. The scene is further embellished after nearly every winter storm by hardy trees plastered with wind-driven snow like so many lonesome statues.

Coleman Pinnacle is a sharp spike in the long spine of Ptarmigan Ridge, situated between Artist Point and Mount Baker. The pinnacle reigns over excellent powder bowls and runs that are over 1,000 vertical feet long. The tour to the pinnacle passes through several highly avalanche-prone areas and is unsafe unless the snow is quite stable. Be sure and talk with the Forest Service snow ranger at the ski area before heading out.

Access: Drive Highway 542 east from Bellingham 55 miles to its end at the upper Mount Baker Ski Area parking lot (4,120 feet). (On Mondays and

Mount Baker from Kulshan Ridge

Tuesdays the road is not plowed.) Park with the downhill skiers and head out. There has been some attempt by the ski area to collect a parking fee from cross-country skiers. The area owners can charge a fee for parking in their lot, but they cannot charge for parking along the road.

Artist Point: From the south end of the upper parking lot, head along the edge of the ski area, following the summer road to Austin Pass. Stay out of the path of the downhillers. (You may pass by the cross-country skiers fee box with a clear conscience; you are heading far beyond the limits of the ski area.)

Follow the road along the west side of the beginners' chairlifts to a broad bench at the ski area boundary. Here folks with climbing skins will zip past their herringboning and kick-turning comrades. Stay to the right of the road until you reach the ridge crest at Austin Pass (4,700 feet). Bear right along the ridge. Skiers with climbing skins can take the quick route, straight up the next hill. Others will contour east on the road to gentler slopes, then head left and climb the rolling terrain to the crest of Kulshan Ridge (4,900 feet). Be wary of the drop-off on the far side—don't let enthusiasm for the view draw you beyond the trees that mark the edge of the ridge.

Telemarker descending from Artist Point

To the right are the imposing cliffs of Table Mountain, so turn left and follow Kulshan Ridge to Artist Point, 200 feet higher and ¼ mile farther. Be sure to bring a big lunch because once on Artist Point the hours disappear amid the breathtaking beauty.

Coleman Pinnacle: There are two approaches. The shortest is to ski to Kulshan Ridge (see above). Once on the ridge, climb to the right. Near the base of Table Mountain cross over the ridge and drop nearly 200 vertical feet in a single swoop down the south side, then traverse along the lower edge of the open slope below Table Mountain to a 5,000-foot saddle. This is an area of extreme avalanche danger. Do not attempt to cross below Table Mountain when the snow pack is unstable.

The alternate approach is via Herman Saddle (see Tour 11) and Chain Lakes. This route requires some extra climbing. If the day is a warm one, use Herman Saddle as your return route.

Once beyond Table Mountain, descend to contour below the first hump on Ptarmigan Ridge. Once safely beyond the rocky cliffs head up the ridge and ski along the crest. Following the route of the summer trail, stay on the southeast side as much as possible. The pinnacle is an obvious rocky spur and the fourth major high point encountered along the ridge. Ski east around the pinnacle then head down the bowl on the west side. Snow remains powdery here for much of the season and the run is outstanding.

To return, ski well to the west of the steep slopes of Ptarmigan Ridge.

11 HERMAN SADDLE

Class: *self-propelled*
Rating: *backcountry*
Round trip: *5 miles*
Skiing time: *4–6 hours*
Elevation gain: *1,380 feet*

High point: *5,300 feet*
Best: *December–April*
Avalanche potential: *moderate*
Map: *Green Trails, Mt. Shuksan No. 14*

See map on page 43

The Herman Saddle tour offers some of the finest downhill cross-country skiing in the western Cascades. The snow is frequently powdery and light and the slopes are often smoother than most groomed ski areas. Views of Mount Shuksan and Mount Baker are huge beyond Table Mountain—and the entire tour is in plain view of lift skiers on Panorama Dome.

Note: Avalanches are very common on the route, which should not be attempted after a heavy snowfall or during times of unseasonably warm weather. In addition, the route is easily lost in times of poor visibility. Always consult the snow ranger at the ski area before setting out.

Access: Drive to the Mount Baker Ski Area (4,120 feet). Begin as for Artist Point (see Tour 10).

The Tour: Follow the road along the edge of the ski area for ¼ mile. When you reach the steep hill below Austin Pass go right and drop to the old warming hut (a small old log building overlooking Bagley Lakes). From the old warming hut descend left along a sloping bench to its end. A couple of quick turns will bring you to the white plain below, where the two Bagley Lakes lie hidden under a blanket of snow. See how avalanches have swept across this little basin and contemplate the foolhardiness of skiing here during periods of instability.

Coyote tracks in the snow

Skiers descending open slopes below Herman Saddle

Cross the basin and head for Herman Saddle, the lowest and most obvious pass in the circle of peaks between Table Mountain and Mazama Dome.
As the basin bends west, the ascent begins. Skiers with climbing skins will
be glad; for those without, a long series of switchbacks commences to gain
the next 800 feet. Stay to the right, on the flanks of Mount Herman, well away
from the basin headwall. Near the top, at around 5,100 feet, head left (south),
contouring below Mazama Dome to reach the saddle at 5,300 feet. On the
way up plan your descent. Decide which slopes you want to mark with
graceful figure-8s (or sitzmarks) for lift skiers on Panorama Dome to admire
and envy (or laugh at).

12 FINNEY CREEK

Class: *multiple use*
Rating: *more difficult*
Round trip: *5–14 miles*
Skiing time: *2–8 hours*
Elevation gain: *500–2,200 feet*

High point: *4,400 feet*
Best: *January–March*
Avalanche potential: *low–moderate*
Map: *USFS, Darrington RD*

Finney Creek is an area you must visit when snow covered and only when snow covered. During the summer months, Finney Creek valley looks like a discarded stage setting for King Kong met Godzilla. However, when the clearcuts and stumps are covered with a soft cloak of white, the valley magically transforms into a winter wonderland with miles of roads to ski, clearcuts to telemark, and sweeping views of the North Cascades to admire.

In addition to the mainline logging road, which opens the entire Finney Creek valley for exploration, four of the spur roads make excellent winter tours. The first spur starts at a very low elevation and the last is quite high, allowing skiers to follow the snowline up the valley from midwinter right into springtime.

Access: Drive Highway 20 to the sign marking the western city limits of Concrete (don't be confused by a store/service station complex on the outskirts). Turn right on Concrete–Sauk Valley Road and follow it across the Skagit River and upstream. At 10 miles from Highway 20 turn right on Finney Creek Road No. 17, a one-lane paved road with turnouts.

The Tour: When the snow has descended all the way to the valley floor, find a place to park out of the way of any traffic and ski up the road. After 3 miles of gradual but steady climbing the road reaches a bench with excellent views over the valley (790 feet). This is a great turnaround point; beyond, the road meanders slowly up-valley and is best if driven to one of the following spur roads.

Road 1705: At 8 miles from the valley floor find Road 1705 on the right (1,200 feet). This spur road switchbacks 7 miles to the 3,800-foot crest of Leonards Ridge and a spectacular view of Baker, Shuksan, and mountains up and down the Skagit. Bring the Forest Service Ranger District map to identify them all. Numerous spur roads branch off Road 1705. Stay left at 1½ miles, right at 2⅓ miles, and left at 3 miles. At the crest of Leonards Ridge the road divides again. Go right on Road 1709 for a cruise along the ridge top.

Road 1720: At 10.5 miles up Finney Creek Road find Gee Point Road No. 1720 on the right (1,600 feet). This road winds more than 10 miles into the

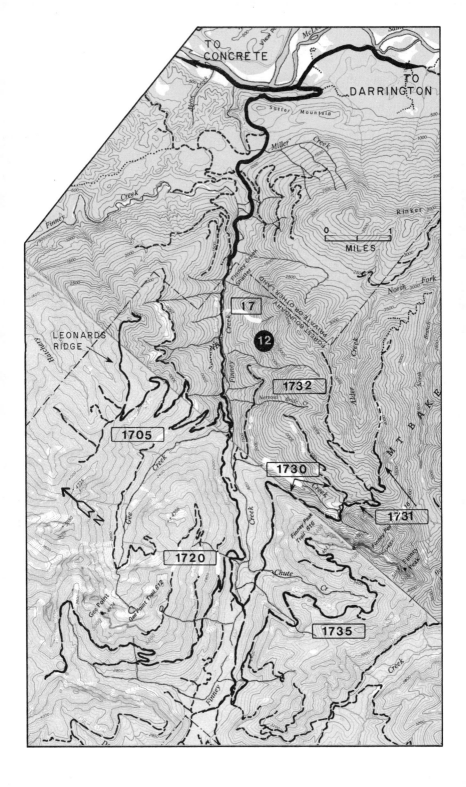

Skiing across a clearcut slope above Finney Creek

mountains, climbing to 4,200 feet on the side of Gee Point. Once again it is a good idea to carry a Forest Service Ranger District map to help you through the intersections. If you stick with Road 1720 the entire distance you will end up on a saddle overlooking the Pressentin Creek drainage.

Road 1730: At 11.8 miles (that is 0.3 mile after crossing Finney Creek), find Road 1730 on the left. This is the most scenic of the four spurs. Starting at 1,800 feet Road 1730 climbs steadily while traversing under the impressive face of Finney Peak. At 6 miles the road divides; go right on Road 1731. In just ¾ mile the road divides again; stay right, still on Road 1731. A final ¼-mile climb leads to the crest of a 4,400-foot knoll where the views encompass all the North Cascades from Whitehorse to the Sisters. This road crosses several avalanche chutes and should not be attempted during periods of snow instability.

Road 1735: At 13 miles up Finney Creek Road find Road 1735 on the left. This road climbs 7 miles to a basin (4,200 feet) on the west side of Finney Peak.

13 SAUK MOUNTAIN

Class: *multiple use*
Rating: *most difficult*
Round trip: *up to 12 miles*
Skiing time: *6 hours*
Elevation gain: *up to 3,525 feet*

High point: *4,000 feet*
Best: *January–February*
Avalanche potential: *high beyond mile 6*
Maps: *Green Trails, Lake Shannon No. 46 and Darrington No. 78*

Difficult, possibly dangerous, and very beautiful is the best way to describe a ski tour up Sauk Mountain Road. Difficult: The road is very steep and can be extremely challenging when icy. Possibly dangerous: The road crosses several avalanche chutes. When the snow is unstable you should turn around at the 6-mile point. Very beautiful: The panorama of North Cascade summits viewed from the high bowls and ridge crests will bring you back time and again.

Access: Drive Highway 20 east toward Rockport State Park. At 0.1 mile west of the park turn north onto Sauk Mountain Road No. 1030 and drive to the snowline. The tour description starts from Highway 20 (475 feet), although skiing generally starts up higher.

The Tour: If you are lucky enough to start skiing at Highway 20, the climb is gentle as the road heads due north through heavy timber. Near the end of the first mile, enter a large clearcut where the real climb begins. Near 1½

Avalanches frequently sweep across the upper portion of Sauk Mountain Road.

miles the road forks at the corner of a switchback. Take the left fork, completing the switchback. Continue a zigzag ascent to the top of the clearing.

After 3 miles the road reenters the forest but continues climbing steadily. The good views begin at the 6-mile point, when you momentarily break out of the trees to look over the Sauk River valley toward Suiattle Mountain, Glacier Peak, and the Puget Lowlands.

The road heads east, skirting the base of Sauk Mountain—above are the avalanche chutes, descending the 2,000 feet from the summit in a single long drop. If the avalanche potential is medium or high, turn around here (3,400 feet).

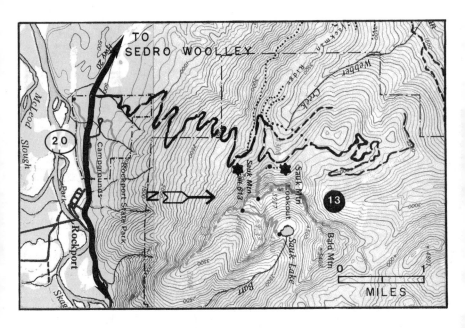

The road traverses the base of Sauk Mountain, then swings away in a final long switchback, returning to the mountain at mile 7, where a major intersection marks an ideal turnaround point (3,900 feet). To continue stay right and follow Sauk Mountain Road as it climbs to 4,000 feet then crosses across an open and extremely hazardous basin. Do not continue on to the ridge tops beyond if the snow is unstable or the weather is unseasonably warm.

HIGHWAY 20

14 PARK BUTTE

Class: *multiple use*
Rating: *backcountry*
Round trip: *up to 18 miles*
Skiing time: *1–3 days*
Elevation gain: *3,100 feet*

High point: *5,000 feet*
Best: *March–May*
Avalanche potential: *moderate*
Maps: *Green Trails, Lake Shannon No. 46 and Hamilton No. 45*

By springtime, a single day is ample time to reach the snow-covered meadows of Park Butte and return to the car before dark. However, a single day is not enough time to ski each and every inviting slope at the Butte and on the adjoining flanks of Mount Baker. Carry camping gear to ensure

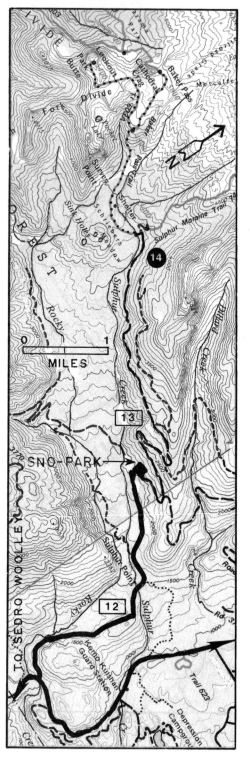

sufficient time to ski all the snow-covered meadows, then climb a hill to watch the sunset over Twin Sisters.

Sad to say, the wide-open spaces attract snow machines like a picnic does ants. Until the Forest Service recognizes that this spectacular area is the wrong place for motorized rodeo, skiers will be happier if they visit late in the season or on a weekday.

Access: Drive Highway 20 east from Sedro Woolley 14.5 miles and go left on Baker Lake Road. At 12.5 miles, just after crossing Rocky Creek, turn left on Loomis–Nooksack Road No. 12. The road is drivable throughout the winter for 3.5 miles to a Sno-Park at the junction of Loomis–Nooksack Road and Schriebers Meadow Road No. 13 (1,900 feet). Hopefully you will be able to drive on up Road 13. The ideal time to ski is when you can drive 4 of the 5 miles to the trailhead.

The Tour: Five miles from the Sno-Park, Road 13 ends at the Park Butte Trailhead. Follow the well-signed, heavily traveled snowmobile track across Sulphur Creek and stick with it for the next ¼ mile to Schriebers Meadow (3,263 feet).

Skier crossing Park Butte; Black Buttes in distance

Follow Sulphur Creek to the upper end of the meadow. Continue to use the creek as a guide and head up the open slope between two lateral moraines left by the receding Easton Glacier. About halfway up the first rise you will be faced with at least one creek crossing—use caution during the spring melt season. Ski up the middle of the valley to the last tree. You now should be opposite the highest point of the moraine on your right. Go left and traverse the relatively gentle slope to the top of the moraine on the left (climbing skins are handy if you have them). Follow the crest of the moraine for 100 feet, then ski through trees to a small gully which, when followed to the top (4,500 feet), gives views over the entire area.

Skier on moraine; Mount Baker in distance

On a clear day you will see the endless slopes to ski here and to the east; enjoy.

Park Butte Lookout is maintained by the Skagit Alpine Club. The building is open throughout the winter and available to visitors on a first-come basis. No system for preregistration is available at this time (95/96 season) so an alternate shelter should always be carried. Reservations may be required in the future—check with the Mount Baker Ranger Station for more information. The final approach to the lookout is steep and can be dangerous when icy.

15 ANDERSON BUTTE

Class: multiple use
Rating: more difficult
Round trip: 10 miles
Skiing time: 5 hours
Elevation gain: 2,000 feet

High point: 4,500 feet
Best: mid-March–April
Avalanche potential: low
Map: Green Trails, Lake Shannon No. 46

Oh, what a view! Save this trip for a clear day when you can abandon the briefcase and the pinstripes for your skis and lycra. To really savor the views bring along a sun hat and your lawn chair. If you prefer catching your views on the run, bring the metal edged skis and carve up the clearcuts.

Access: Follow Highway 20 east from Sedro Woolley 14.5 miles and turn left on Baker Lake–Grandy Lake Road. Drive to the Baker Dam turnoff and go right on Road 1106. Pass a campground at 1.3 miles, then cross the dam. At 2.2 miles from Baker Lake Road, turn left onto Road 1107 and follow signs towards Watson Lakes Trail.

As the snowline varies, there is no way to predict the starting location, but in early or late season much of the slog up the lower portion of the road can be avoided. Trip mileages start at the Road 1107 intersection, but with

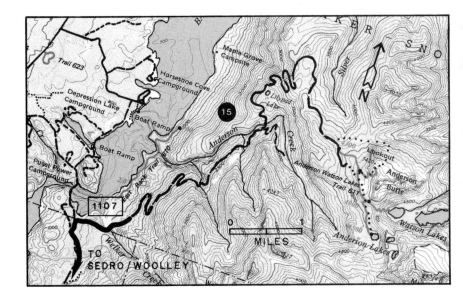

Mount Baker from Anderson Butte Road

planning and a bit of luck you should be able to drive 4 or 5 miles beyond the turnoff, to around 2,500 feet.

The Tour: From snowline, ski up Road 1107, crossing Anderson Creek 5½ miles from Road 1106 and passing Lilypad Lake near 6 miles (3,000 feet). Soon after, Mount Baker comes into full view, complete with an occasional wisp of pungent steam from Sherman Crater.

The road heads into a series of switchbacks culminating at 8¼ miles (3,850 feet) when Mount Shuksan, looking like a centerfold photograph, commands your attention. It doesn't get any better than this, so if you've got the lawn chair in tow, plunk it down and enjoy.

If lounging isn't your style, continue on. The road winds over a gentle ridge at 8½ miles where you'll obtain your first views of Anderson Butte and the glaciated mass of Bacon Peak beyond. Just ahead is a huge, north-facing clearcut which frequently holds good powder, long after the neighboring slopes have turned into slurpies. Pick a slope with a view of Mount Baker or Mount Shuksan to practice the fine art of simultaneous view watching and telemarking.

16 MOUNT SHUKSAN

Class: self-propelled
Rating: mountaineer
Round trip: 11 miles
Skiing time: 8 hours
Elevation gain: 6,000 feet

High point: 8,400 feet
Best: March–May
Avalanche potential: high
Map: USGS, Mt. Shuksan

The south-facing Sulphide Glacier on Mount Shuksan offers a 4,000-foot run over moderate slopes, skiable by experts and the telemark-impaired alike. As if that isn't enough, Sulphide Glacier is an extraordinarily scenic tour with full-on views of Mount Baker, Mount Blum, Bacon Peak, Sauk Mountain, and Glacier Peak, as well as numerous other dignitaries of the North Cascades.

Although the skiing is relatively easy, the numerous natural hazards—like avalanche slopes and crevasses—pose a real threat to the inexperienced. Wands to mark the route in case of bad weather, avalanche beacons, and shovels for every member of the party are necessary pieces of equipment on this mountain.

Access: Drive Highway 20 east from Sedro Woolley 14.5 miles and turn left on Baker Lake–Grandy Lake Road. Drive to the Koma Kulshan Guard Station, then continue on Forest Road 11 for 9.7 miles. Go left on Road 1152

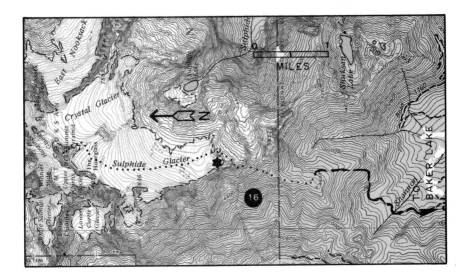

The descent

and head uphill for 0.2 mile before taking the first fork on the right. Drive 3 miles up a series of switchbacks. Turn right on Spur Road 014 and continue on until the road is blocked by brush or snow (up to a mile). Park here (2,400 feet).

The Tour: Ski or hike along the old brush-clogged road. Cross Shannon Creek then head around the shoulder of the hill, to reach the base of a clearcut at 1 mile. Ski or posthole up the hillside to reach the ridge top at 4,600 feet. Next, head north along the ridge following the snow-covered Shannon Ridge

Trail through heavy timber for a short mile to open meadows and campsites.

When the ridge runs into a steep, west-facing slope, turn right (east) and head up the slope to a col on the ridge above. This steep hillside is prone to sliding after heavy snowfall or strong wind or during a warm afternoon.

Cross over the col and make a hazardous, 500-foot traverse across a steep and avalanche-prone slope. Stay on the narrow shelf between two cliff bands. *Note:* This is the most dangerous area encountered on this tour. Do not cross here after a snowfall or in the heat of late afternoon. If in doubt, turn back at the col.

Beyond the cliff, the slope broadens; turn north and ski up to the terminus of Sulphide Glacier. The gradient of the slope rapidly decreases as you climb, and campsites are numerous on the left (west) side of the slope. Head north; slopes will become a bit steeper above 6,600 feet and level off again around 7,200 feet. You are now skiing right up a glacier, so watch for crevasses throughout.

The summit pyramid is very steep and rocky and skied only by the crazed, willing to crash and burn big-time or out-ski the avalanche they generate. Life-loving skiers can contour east around the base of the summit pyramid to the ridge beyond. Turn around at about 8,400 feet.

On the way down follow your ascent route as closely as possible to avoid unseen crevasses and unsuspected cliffs. Remember to head down early to avoid possible slides caused by the afternoon heat.

HIGHWAY 530

17 GREEN MOUNTAIN

Class: *self-propelled*
Rating: *mountaineer*
Round trip: *8 miles from road-end*
Skiing time: *6 hours*
Elevation gain: *3,030 feet*

High point: *6,500 feet*
Best: *December and May*
Avalanche potential: *moderate*
Map: *USGS, Downey Mtn.*

Because of a long road approach and high avalanche potential throughout the winter, Green Mountain is best reserved for early- or late-season tours. As soon as the emerald meadows are covered by 2 feet of snow, skiing is excellent on the steep, open slopes amid views of the North Cascades from Baker to Rainier. In spring the timing is trickier. A party must wait until the road opens and the snow pack stabilizes to solid corn, but not so long that the snow is more water than snow—or has gone into summer hibernation. The timing for views, however, is not difficult to figure. It just takes good weather.

Access: Drive north from Darrington or south from Rockport to Suiattle River Road No. 26 and follow it 19 miles to Green Mountain Road No. 2680 (1,300 feet). Head up 5 miles to the road-end (3,500 feet) or until blocked by snow or slides.

The Tour: The Green Mountain Trail starts on a forested hillside 300 feet before the road-end. Ski or hike the steep trail. After a mile in dense timber the trail reaches treeline at the edge of open meadows (4,200 feet). (If the trail is lost in timber, ski steeply up from the parking lot with a slight lean to the left.)

At treeline skirt left around the edge of the meadows, keeping in the shelter of the trees and avoiding several obvious avalanche tracks. At the end of the meadows turn uphill and climb, in the protection of the trees, 200 feet to a slanting bench.

Glacier Peak from the Green Mountain ski route

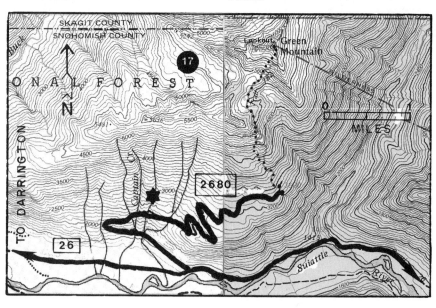

Green Mountain

Traverse to the right using as much forest cover as possible. Once on the east side of the slope, ski on up to the ridge top. Follow the crest up another 500 feet then traverse right to a tree-dotted shelf leading to a deep bowl which holds a small snow-covered lake (5,220 feet).

Before reaching the lake look ahead and choose your route to the lookout on the 6,500-foot summit of Green Mountain. When the snow is stable, ski up the middle of the open slope to the first saddle west of the lookout. Once on the saddle, follow the ridge to the summit. When the snow is unstable, the only way to the top is via the northwest ridge. On top, unwrap the sandwiches and gaze at Mount Buckindy (just to the north), Dome Peak, Baker, and Shuksan. To the south stand Glacier Peak, White Chuck, Pugh, and Sloan.

North Mountain Lookout

18 NORTH MOUNTAIN ROAD

Class: *multiple use*
Rating: *more difficult*
Round trip: *2–28 miles*
Skiing time: *2 hours–2 days*
Elevation gain: *up to 3,000 feet*

High point: *4,000 feet*
Best: *January–April*
Avalanche potential: *low*
Map: *Green Trails, Darrington No. 78*

North Mountain Road yields views of lazy, damp valley bottoms as well as crisp polar displays of Whitehorse, Higgins, Pugh, Glacier Peak, White Chuck, Baker, and the Pickets.

Snow in the North Mountain area is an extremely variable commodity.

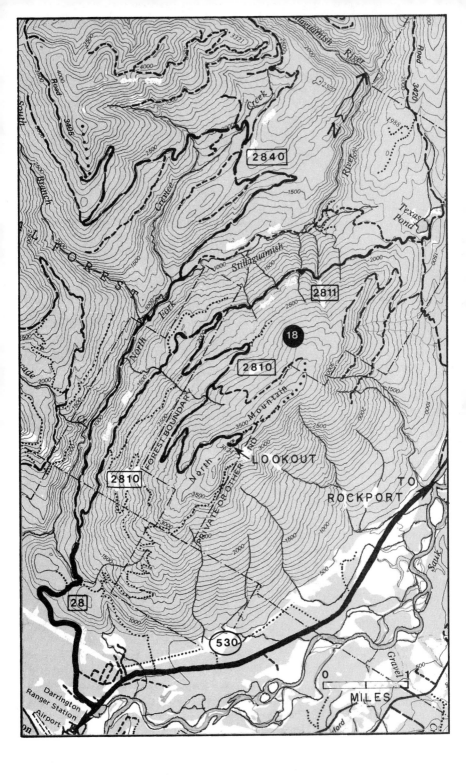

Trips in this area may start at the valley floor or high on the ridge crests. Luckily, the numerous roads that branch off of the mainline provide destinations suitable for whatever amount of time is available, wherever the snowline may be.

Access: Drive Highway 530 to Darrington. Continue north on the highway 0.7 mile past the Darrington Ranger Station then turn left on paved Road 28. At 2.5 miles is a major intersection (1,000 feet), the usual midwinter starting point for skiers.

The Tour: The right fork, Road 2810, heads toward Texas Pond and North Mountain Lookout and is the recommended route when the machine-sitting crowd is not out in force. Ski 3½ miles, gaining 1,000 feet, then take a right and switchback another 6½ miles up to open slopes and a tremendous viewpoint at the 3,824-foot lookout. In winter this is an overnight destination; in March and April, when the road can be driven farther, it's an easy day.

For shorter trips or on days when the machines are marauding, take the lower left fork from the 1,000-foot intersection. This road remains at a near-constant elevation for 4 miles to the crossing of North Fork Stillaguamish River. In ¼ mile more the road splits. The left fork, Road 2840, winds 12 miles up to an end on a 4,000-foot ridge top. Clearcuts along the way provide a succession of vistas; views from the top are superb.

HIGHWAY 530

19 SEGELSEN CREEK ROAD

Class: *multiple use*
Rating: *more difficult*
Round trip: *up to 24 miles*
Skiing time: *2 hours–2 days*
Elevation gain: *up to 3,011 feet*

High point: *3,431 feet at Deer Creek Pass*
Best: *January–April*
Avalanche potential: *low*
Map: *Green Trails, Darrington No. 78*

A week could be spent skiing here without covering the whole Segelsen Creek area. As with all roads that start at low elevations, Segelsen Creek has an extremely variable snowline. Depending on whims of the weather, skiers from January through March may start at the absolute bottom—or 5 miles up. Only the spring skier can reasonably hope to drive more than the first few miles. However, the skiing is fun and the views are good no matter where the capricious snowline is.

Access: Drive Highway 530 east from Arlington 24 miles to the small community of Whitehorse. Just opposite the Whitehorse Mercantile (gas station

Rain forest on lower Segelsen Creek Road

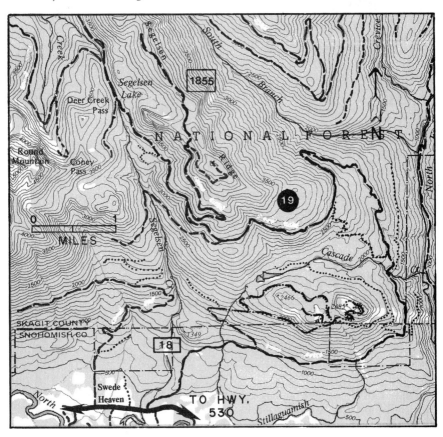

Whitehorse Mountain from Segelsen Creek Road

and store) turn left on Swede Heaven Road, crossing the railroad tracks and bridge. After 1.7 miles go right on Segelsen Creek Road No. 18. Trip mileages in the following description start from this intersection (420 feet).

The Tour: The way climbs through a tunnel of moss-covered trees. Ignore all signs proclaiming this to be a private road. The public *does* have legal access here. At 2 miles a spur road heads sharply back left. Continue straight. Be sure to reach at least one clearcut for views across the valley to glacier-carved Whitehorse Mountain.

The most awesome views start near the 9-mile point and continue for the next 3 miles to Segelsen Creek Road's 3,431-foot high point at Deer Creek Pass. Sit back and absorb views of innumerable peaks, some of them recognizable favorites like Glacier Peak, White Chuck, Whitehorse, Bedal, and Pugh, and some less famous peaks that appear quite distinguished in their winter whites.

An alternate trip for spring skiers is Segelsen Ridge Road. Take a right fork off Road 18 at 9½ miles (3,250 feet) and follow Road 1855 steeply up for 1½ miles to the 4,300-foot ridge crest. Skim along the ridge top for 2 miles of limitless views.

20 WHITE CHUCK MOUNTAIN VIEW

Class: *multiple use*
Rating: *more difficult*
Round trip: *10 miles*
Skiing time: *6 hours*
Elevation gain: *2,350 feet*

High point: *4,450 feet*
Best: *March–April*
Avalanche potential: *low*
Map: *Green Trails, Sloan Peak No. 111*

Ski to endless views of mountains, farms, and clearcuts from a 4,450-foot ridgecrest viewpoint.

Access: Drive Highway 530 to Darrington then, at a T intersection at the center of town, take a right on the Mountain Loop Highway. After 9.4 miles, go left on Road 22, which immediately crosses the White Chuck River and heads back down the valley. After 3.8 miles, go right on Road 24 and head up. Road 24 arrives at a three-way intersection after 4.3 miles of steady climbing. Go straight on Road 2430 for 0.5 mile to an intersection with Road 2435 (2,100 feet). Miles and elevation gain are calculated from this junction, but drive on to the snowline.

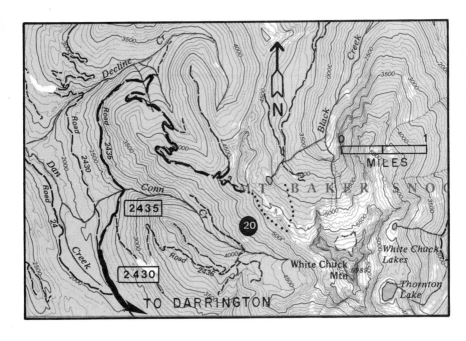

Road 2435 and White Chuck Mountain in distance

The Tour: From the intersection go right and head up through forests and clearcuts on Road 2435. After ½ mile pass Road 2436 (summer climbing access to White Chuck Mountain) on the right (2,700 feet). At 2½ miles a spur road on the left marks the beginning of a series of steep switchbacks. The road arrives at the very narrow ridge crest which divides the Conn Creek drainage to the south from the Decline Creek drainage to the north at the 4½-mile point.

Ascend the narrow crest of the ridge to within a few feet of a 4,450-foot high point. The vista is outstanding and the views feature a host of well-known North Cascade dignitaries including Mount Baker and The Sisters to the north; Higgins, Whitehorse, and Three Fingers to the west; and the Monte Cristo Peaks, Sloan, Pugh, and the towering cliffs of White Chuck Mountain (6,989 feet) to the south.

The road then descends 100 feet, swings north, and contours at a nearly constant elevation for another 2 miles to the end of a ridge overlooking Decline Creek.

21 RAT TRAP PASS

Class: *multiple use*
Rating: *more difficult*
Round trip: *7 miles*
Skiing time: *4 hours*
Elevation gain: *1,492 feet*

High point: *3,150 feet*
Best: *November–December and March*
Avalanche potential: *moderate*
Map: *Green Trails, Sloan Peak No. 111*

Rat Trap is an inelegant name for a beautiful pass boxed in by walls that rise almost straight up for 4,000 feet to the snow-plastered summit of White Chuck Mountain. The pass is ¼ mile of open meadows surrounded by broad clearcut slopes, making it an ideal area for gazing at the views, picnicking, building snowmen, and telemarking.

Timing is crucial for this trip. It is best to plan this tour either in early winter or early spring. Midwinter skiers may, depending on the snowfall, be faced with a long valley-bottom approach of 5½ miles or more up White River Road from the Mountain Loop Highway.

Access: From Darrington drive the Mountain Loop Highway south 9.5 miles then turn left on White River Road No. 23. Head up-valley 5.5 miles and park at the Road 2700 junction (1,668 feet).

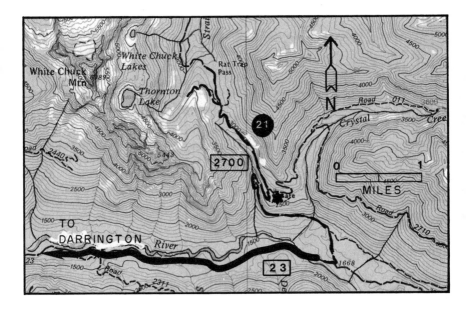

White Chuck Mountain from Rat Trap Pass

The Tour: Ski up Road 2700, climbing gradually. Two spur roads are passed in the first ¾ mile; stay left both times. At 1¼ miles is the first good view of Pugh and an excellent view of Glacier Peak.

Near 2 miles the road enters a narrow valley, twice crosses a boisterous little creek, then winds across a steep open hillside. Snow sloughs from the hillside above after any heavy snowfall so, using caution and common sense, ski briskly across the exposed area.

At 2½ miles, the abandoned Road 2710 branches off to the east for a long level traverse to the Meadow Mountain Trailhead. A mile beyond the intersection, Road 2700 makes a final switchback, then climbs into the clearcut meadows of Rat Trap Pass (3,150 feet).

Excellent vantage points for gazing at White Chuck Mountain are found throughout the pass area, and at the north end are overlooks down the Straight Creek drainage to farms far below. The best views are at the top of the clearcut hill on the west side of the pass. To reach this vantage point, either head straight up the hill or follow Spur Road 016 from its starting point at the entrance to the pass. Once on top you can lay back and watch the avalanches stream down the face of White Chuck Mountain.

22 KENNEDY HOT SPRINGS

Class: *self-propelled*
Rating: *backcountry*
Round trip: *10 miles from road-end*
Skiing time: *8 hours*
Elevation gain: *1,000 feet*

High point: *3,300 feet*
Best: *February–March*
Avalanche potential: *high*
Maps: *Green Trails, Sloan Peak*
    No. 111 and Glacier Peak No. 112

Hot springs and snow are a seductive combination, so it's not surprising that Kennedy Hot Springs is a popular winter destination. A long soak in the hot springs after a day of skiing soothes the back and takes the boredom out of winter camping.

There is no *best time* to ski to Kennedy Hot Springs. If the snowfall has been heavy, the access road may be covered with snow for the entire 11 miles up the White Chuck River valley. When the snowfall has been light, the road may be drivable right to the trailhead and then you may have to walk some or all of the trail. In fact, it is a good idea to throw the hiking boots in the trunk before you leave home, just in case.

Access: Drive to Darrington and follow the "Mountain Loop Highway" signs south. The county road turns into Forest Road No. 20 at the edge of town and parallels the Sauk River. Take the second road on the

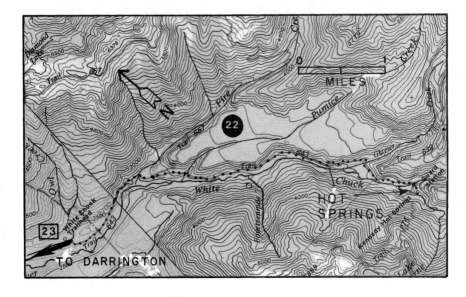

Kennedy Hot Springs

left immediately after crossing the Sauk River bridge. White Chuck River Road No. 23 is 11 miles long and ends at the trailhead (2,300 feet).

The Tour: The trail travels upriver, tunneling through thick brush and around tall trees for ¾ mile before climbing along a steep hillside above the river. At 1½ miles, descend to cross Fire Creek where Meadow Mountain Trail is passed. After crossing Pumice Creek at 2 miles, descend to the river and traverse a beach area covered with boulders freshly dislodged from the hillside above. Do not linger in this hazardous area.

Shortly beyond, the trail crosses a steep, slide-prone bank that ends in the river. Snow sloughs frequently on this sidehill. If the trail is snow covered, do not cross. Instead, retreat 100 feet or so and scramble up a broad slope to the top of the terrace. Cross over the top of the slide area then return to the trail. A little farther on there is a second hazardous bank. This one must be crossed. Take off your skis and walk.

A solitary switchback provides a notable landmark at 4 miles. Beyond this single twist the trail enters an open flood plain where several creeks are crossed. Kennedy Creek, at the far end of the plain, is the final creek. After the last crossing, go right along the base of a forested hill to reach the guard station at 5 miles (3,300 feet). The best camping is located in this area.

The hot springs pool is located on the opposite side of the White Chuck River and reached by a bridge. Cross with caution as the only handrail, located on the upriver side, is frequently hidden under a mound of snow.

Once across go left 50 feet to the steaming pool, which is fairly warm through the winter (it does cool off during the spring snowmelt).

Don't just stand there, hop in.

MOUNTAIN LOOP HIGHWAY—VERLOT AREA

23 MOUNT PILCHUCK

Class: self-propelled
Rating: most difficult
Round trip: 14 miles
Skiing time: 6 hours
Elevation gain: 2,120 feet

High point: 3,120 feet
Best: January–February
Avalanche potential: low
Map: Green Trails, Granite Falls No. 109

In the early 1970s Mount Pilchuck was the scene of bustling winter activity. Skiers drove bumper to bumper up a narrow winding road for 7 horrific miles to ski one of Washington's most challenging downhill runs. Lodge sitters, avoiding the embarrassments of cliff skiing, were rewarded for their lack of effort with an excellent view across the Robe Valley to 6,854-foot Three Fingers.

Today the ski lifts and crowds of downhill skiers have gone, beaten by poor weather and difficult terrain. However, the views and an excellent road for ski touring remain. Best of all, the road, after the first 1½ miles, is reserved all winter for nonmotorized use. The parking area at the top makes a comfortable and scenic campsite and the once-groomed slope below is ideal for a little downhill-telemark practice. (The more challenging slopes above the road-end may also be skied; however, the avalanche potential is very high above 3,600 feet.)

Access: Drive the Mountain Loop Highway 1 mile east of the Verlot Public Service Center. Immediately after crossing the South Fork Stillaguamish

Three Fingers Mountain from the old Mount Pilchuck downhill ski area

River, turn right on Pilchuck Road No. 42. If the road is snowfree, drive 1.5 miles to a gate and park (1,400 feet). If the road is blocked or partially blocked by snow return to the bottom and park along the Mountain Loop Highway. Do not block the access to private property by parking on one of the spur roads.

The Tour: Pilchuck Road climbs steadily, passing several spur roads. After 5 miles the road levels somewhat and starts into a long switchback that ends 2 scenic miles later at the parking lot.

Skiers wishing to climb higher will find easy access across the old ski slope above the road-end parking area. An old service road begins a short way up the slope on the right, winds through the trees, and reemerges just below the summit of the first hill. Beyond this point the route is difficult, ascending steep slopes and a short cliff to the top of the old ski area. The

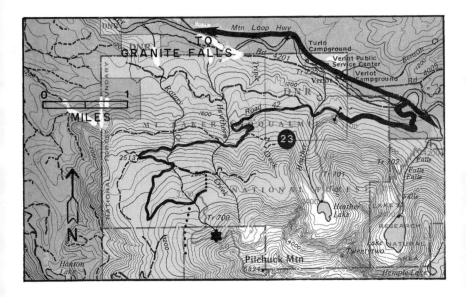

avalanche hazard rises dramatically as you go up. Ski ascents of 5,324-foot Pilchuck are fraught with danger and not worth the risk.

On the way back, consider a shortcut down the old ski slope below the end of the road. Near the base of the slope go left on an overgrown logging spur and bushwhack back to rejoin the main road just above the 5-mile marker.

MOUNTAIN LOOP HIGHWAY—VERLOT AREA

24 SCHWEITZER CREEK LOOP

Class: multiple use
Rating: most difficult
Round trip: 11½ miles
Skiing time: 8 hours
Elevation gain: 1,800 feet

High point: 2,800 feet
Best: January–February
Avalanche potential: low
Map: Green Trails, Silverton No. 110

Day trips, overnight trips, side trips, and loop trips—they're all here. Take as much time as you can spare to fully explore this area or plan to come back several times.

The Schweitzer Creek Road system attracts a full complement of the winter users: snowshoers, hikers, dogsleds, three-wheelers, four-wheelers, snowmobiles. Don't discount the skiing altogether, though. The parade can be entertaining and the skiing, especially during midweek, is very good.

Note: The ¼-mile connector trail that completes the loop has not been maintained for the last five years. The route is becoming overgrown and some of the markers have disappeared. If you are unfamiliar with this area you may have trouble following the trail. First-time visitors should approach this loop with a sense of adventure. Do not be afraid to turn back if you become confused.

Access: Drive east from Granite Falls on the Mountain Loop Highway 11 miles to the Verlot Public Service Center. Check your odometer and continue on another 3.9 miles to Schweitzer Creek Road No. 4020 (1,200 feet).

The Tour: The road starts off with an intersection. Stay to the right and begin the climb out of the rain-forest environment of the valley floor. Several spur roads are passed before reaching the intersection that marks the beginning of the loop portion of the tour at 2¾ miles (2,150 feet). Go left, continuing straight ahead on Road 4020.

The views are excellent as the road traverses clearcut hillsides. Look for Big Four Mountain as well as Vesper, Sperry, and Three Fingers. Near 5 miles, the road rounds a steep switchback. Immediately after watch on the left for the Lake Evan Trail. The lake is located only a few hundred feet from the

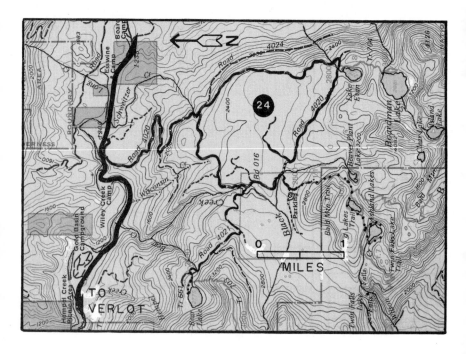

Clearcuts can provide excellent skiing.

road (2,751 feet). No campsites exist here. Good tent sites may be found by following the trail for another mile to Boardman Lake if you are willing to cross a slippery logjam to reach them. If not, consider pitching your tent in the trailhead parking area.

To continue the loop, follow Road 4020 on up the hillside. The road levels off at 2,800 feet (near mile 5½) then descends gently for 1 mile through a brush-covered clearcut. Continue on for ⅛ mile after the road returns to the trees then watch on the left for a blue diamond and, maybe, a sign marking the faint trail. Head left, through the grove of venerable old trees to a clearcut, then continue straight ahead to find the Ashland Lakes Trail in ¼ mile.

At the Ashland Lakes Trail you are faced with another choice. To the left (south) you may follow the trail ¼ mile to a campsite at the old Ashland Lakes Trailhead or follow the trail into the backcountry for 1 mile to Beaver Plant Lake (2,900 feet) or 1½ miles to the two Ashland Lakes. Campsites may be found at all the lakes. To continue the loop head right (north) on the Ashland Lakes Trail ½ mile to an intersection and new trailhead parking.

Go left on the road for a short, steep, descent to reach Road 4021 at 7 miles (2,400 feet).

Road 4021 offers another chance for a side trip. Just 1¾ miles to the left is the Bear Lake Trailhead (2,600 feet), where a ¼-mile trail leads to the forested lake and more campsites.

The loop follows Road 4021 to the right (north) contouring around the flat-topped ridge to views of Three Fingers and Mount Pilchuck. At 9 miles Road 4021 meets road 4020 and ends, closing the loop portion of the tour. Go left and descend back to the Mountain Loop Highway at 11½ miles.

MOUNTAIN LOOP HIGHWAY—VERLOT AREA

25 MALLARDY RIDGE

Class: multiple use
Rating: more difficult
Round trip: 12 miles
Skiing time: 6 hours
Elevation gain: 2,300 feet

High point: 3,600 feet
Best: January–February
Avalanche potential: low
Map: Green Trails, Silverton No. 110

Ski from a delicate world of moss-hung trees on the valley floor to a wind-blown winterland on Mallardy Ridge. This is a popular multiple-use area and weekend visitors must expect to share these forest roads with all other

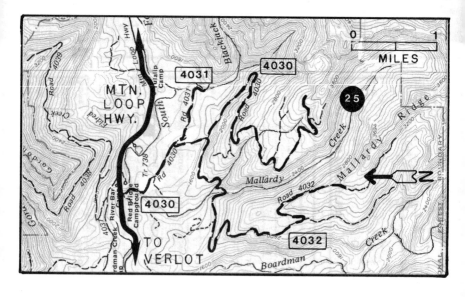

Mount Pilchuck from Road 4030

known forms of winter recreation, including jeeps, snowmobiles, and UFOs (Unidentified Fuming Objects), as well as hikers, snowshoers, rabbits, and coyotes. For peace, ski here during the middle of the week.

Access: Drive east from the Verlot Public Service Center 7.2 miles on the Mountain Loop Highway. Just before the road crosses Red Bridge look for a small pull-off on the right signed "Mallardy Ridge Road." Park along the side of the highway, out of traffic's way. The elevation is very low here (1,300 feet), so make your plans as flexible as the snowline.

The Tour: Mallardy Ridge Road No. 4030 starts off fairly level but soon crosses Mallardy Creek and makes a quick, steep climb to a broad terrace. Avoid all spur roads left and right as you follow the obvious road on a gentle climb for the 1¼ miles to a major intersection and a choice at 1,600 feet.

Mallardy Ridge Road

The road signs here have been hunted to near extinction; however, your map will tell you that Road 4030 is to the left and Road 4032 is to the right. Both roads offer good touring. The left fork, Road 4030, climbs rapidly for 4 miles and ends at 3,600 feet in a clearcut. On the way up you will pass several spur roads. In 1995 the spurs had been abandoned and the main road was easy to follow. From the top are views of Bald Mountain and Gordon Ridge as well as a far-reaching vista to the west. The descent varies from fast to a real screamer when icy.

The right fork, Road 4032, makes a rolling ascent of Mallardy Ridge. Beyond the intersection, the road climbs for ½ mile then descends to cross Mallardy Creek before continuing a steep ascent up the ridge. Several spots along this road are ideal for a scenic lunch with vistas over Boardman and Schweitzer Creeks. Near 5 miles the road crests the ridge. This is the turn-around point when the snow is unstable. In stable conditions, however, you can follow the road across a steep, exposed slope before cutting back to the west side to reach the Mallardy Ridge Trailhead at 6 miles.

26 DEER CREEK ROAD

Class: *self-propelled*
Rating: *more difficult*
Round trip: *9 miles to road-end*
Skiing time: *6 hours*
Elevation gain: *1,500 feet*

High point: *3,100 feet*
Best: *January–March*
Avalanche potential: *low*
Map: *Green Trails, Silverton No. 110*

Deer Creek is one of just two roads in the Verlot area (the other being Mount Pilchuck) reserved for nonmotorized sports. Once past the throngs of enthusiastic snow-players, skiers will find peaceful forest, snow-shrouded clearcuts, and awesome views of knife-edged peaks.

Access: Drive the Mountain Loop Highway east from the Verlot Public Service Center 12.1 miles to the end of plowing at Deer Creek Road No. 4052. Park in the large lot on the left-hand side of the highway (1,600 feet).

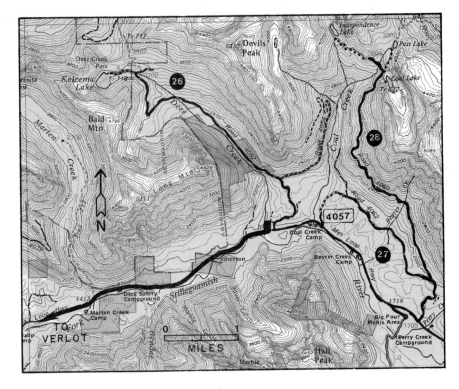

Deer Creek

The Tour: Taking care to dodge exuberant (and sometimes out-of-control) sledders, ski up Deer Creek Road, climbing steeply through dense second growth to a small knob. In the first ½ mile two unsigned spur roads branch off; stay left at both. At 1 mile (2,000 feet) the sadly overgrown Double Eagle Road heads east. Continue left on Deer Creek Road, climbing steadily northwest, deeper into the long, narrow valley. Ahead, Bald Mountain, impressive in its cloak of snow, dominates the skyline.

Views start at 1¼ miles and improve as you climb. By 2¼ miles views have expanded to include the Big Four and the jagged summits of the Monte Cristo group. Near 3½ miles the road crosses Deer Creek and soon after turns abruptly north to ascend along the base of Bald Mountain. Deer Creek is recrossed at the 4½-mile point; immediately after pass the Kelcema Lake Trailhead (3,100 feet). The road continues up through another old clearcut. The return is a long, fun glide.

If you would like a little adventure, ski the forest trail to Kelcema Lake. The lake is located a scant ½ mile from the road and is negotiable by experienced skiers, brave intermediates, and beginners proficient in using tree trunks and branches to slow their descent. The route is not well marked but can be followed to the lake by using Deer Creek as a guide. On the east shore are several sheltered campsites.

MOUNTAIN LOOP HIGHWAY—VERLOT AREA

27 BIG FOUR LOOP

Mountain Loop Highway

Class: multiple use
Rating: easiest
Round trip: 5 miles to picnic area
Skiing time: 3 hours
Elevation gain: 180 feet
High point: 1,780 feet
Best: January–February
Avalanche potential: none
Map: Green Trails, Silverton No. 110

Coal Creek Loop

Class: mostly multiple use
Rating: most difficult
Round trip: 6 miles
Skiing time: 4 hours
Elevation gain: 400 feet
High point: 2,000 feet
Best: January–February
Avalanche potential: low
Map: Green Trails, Silverton No. 110

See map on page 85

The Mountain Loop Highway is a splendid valley-bottom tour. The road tunnels through lush forest of moss-hung trees along the edge of the snowbound Stillaguamish River, and on each side the steep valley walls rise to superbly scenic glacier-bound mountains.

A perfect tour? Not quite. Due to the relatively low elevation, quality and quantity of snow cover are extremely variable. Watch the weather and ski here only when the snow level has been down to the 1,500-foot level for a week or more.

This is a multiple-use area and midwinter the multiples arrive in force:

A frozen stream

dog sleds mush, snowshoers wend, hikers slog, skiers glide, snowmobiles roar, and ATVs skid. If there is too much competition, skiers comfortable with *more difficult* trails can make a traffic-escaping loop via Coal Lake Road.

Access: Drive the Mountain Loop Highway east from the Verlot Public Service Center 12.1 miles to the end of plowing at Deer Creek Road No. 4052. Park in the large lot on the left-hand side of the highway (1,600 feet).

Mountain Loop Highway: From the parking area head east up the Mountain Loop Highway. Skiing should start at the road block that may or may not stop the traffic from continuing up the valley. After ½ mile cross Coal Creek (loop skiers will return to the main road at this point). The road to Big Four Picnic Area branches off to the right after 2½ nearly level miles. The picnic area is a natural turnaround point. The meadow that surrounds the parking area, the site of a hotel until 1949, is an excellent play area. Big Four Mountain dominates, tall and cold, and, when the sun touches it, roars with avalanches.

The 1-mile trail to the ice caves is a popular winter walk from the picnic area. If you choose to do this walk, please remember the roaring avalanches mentioned at the end of the last paragraph. The ice caves are formed, in part, by these avalanches and they are common occurrences. Please stop your walk at the edge of the trees. The entrance to the caves is usually blocked by snow and avalanche debris in the winter anyway.

Coal Creek Loop: To return via the loop, continue on up the Mountain Loop Highway a short ⅛ mile beyond the picnic area then turn left on Coal Lake Road No. 4060. Ski up the road for a long ¾ mile then go left on Road 4062. Ski across clearcuts, then over the valley bottom, 2 miles to the road-end. Continue ahead, following a trail marked with blue diamonds through a band of trees to intersect Road 4057. Turn left and descend ¼ mile to return to the highway just above Coal Creek.

When not chopped up by machines, the Mountain Loop Highway makes a good 8-mile ski tour from Big Four Picnic Area to Barlow Pass. Except for a short stretch above Perry Creek, which poses an avalanche hazard in unstable conditions, the road is safe for the entire distance.

MOUNTAIN LOOP HIGHWAY—VERLOT AREA

28 COAL LAKE

Class: multiple use
Rating: most difficult
Round trip: up to 14½ miles
Skiing time: 5 hours–2 days
Elevation gain: 2,160 feet

High point: 3,880 feet
Best: January–April
Avalanche potential: moderate
Map: Green Trails, Silverton No. 110

See map on page 85

The road to Coal Lake does two great things: (1) It escapes the main traffic flow of the Mountain Loop Highway and (2) it leads to fantastic views of peaks from Mount Pilchuck to Sperry Peak. As everywhere throughout

Del Campo Peak from Coal Lake Road

the Stillaguamish Valley, the roar of snow machines echoes, and lonesomeness is not to be expected. However, a backcountry skier with a little adventure in the heart can leave the main thoroughfares and find a day or more of peace at Coal Lake.

Access: Drive the Mountain Loop Highway east from the Verlot Public Service Center 12.1 miles to the end of plowing at Deer Creek Road No. 4052. If space is available, park in the large lot on the left-hand side of the highway (1,600 feet). When the lot is full, park along the road.

The Tour: Ski up the Mountain Loop Highway 2½ nearly level miles. Shortly after passing the turnoff to Big Four Picnic Area go left on Coal Lake Road No. 4060.

The road climbs gradually, first in forest then in clearcuts with vistas of the Stillaguamish Valley and surrounding peaks. The great north wall of Big Four dominates, but other mountains have their say.

A spur road branches off to the right at ½ mile and a second heads off to the left ¼ mile beyond. This second spur is part of the Coal Creek Loop (see Tour 27). From this point, the route is straight forward without routefinding difficulties. Avalanche hazard is low until about the 6¼-mile point, where the road crosses a steep, open slope just before entering into heavy timber. Cross only if the snow is stable. At 6¾ miles pass the Coal Lake Viewpoint. Continue on for a final ¼ mile. Just before the Coal Lake outlet creek, go right to find the lake and campsites a short ⅛ mile from the road (3,420 feet).

For further explorations follow an unmarked path to Pass Lake or follow the road to its end at 7¼ miles (3,680 feet).

29 LAKE ELIZABETH

Class: *multiple use*
Rating: *easiest*
Round trip: *13 miles*
Skiing time: *7 hours*
Elevation gain: *1,930 feet*

High point: *2,850 feet*
Best: *January–February*
Avalanche potential: *low*
Maps: *Green Trails, Skykomish No. 175 and Mt. Si No. 174*

With a starting elevation of 920 feet, this is indisputably a low-elevation tour. But don't be discouraged—the high walls of the valley block out the sun throughout the shortest days of winter, and once the snow falls it lingers for a month or more.

The route to Lake Elizabeth follows a well-graded road up Money Creek

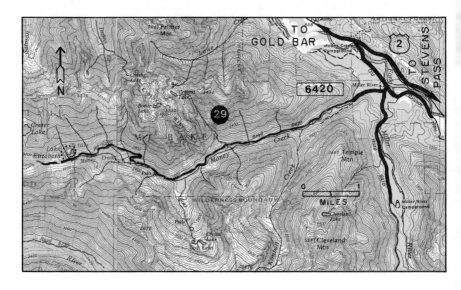

Lake Elizabeth

valley for 6½ miles to the small subalpine lake and several mining claims. This can be a peaceful as well as scenic tour or, on an occasional weekend, it can be a hectic trip where you must slalom ski around the 4x4 trucks, dodge packs of snowmobiles, and jump out of the path of racing dog sleds. Camping possibilities are limited to the area near the lake.

Access: Drive Highway 2 east 17.5 miles from Gold Bar or west 2.7 miles from Skykomish. At the Money Creek Campground sign, turn right (south) and follow the Old Cascade Highway for 1 mile before making a right turn on Miller River Road No. 6410. After 200 feet turn right again on Money Creek Road No. 6420. Drive past the few houses that comprise the community of Miller River to reach, in 0.6 mile, the end of the plowed road at the Money Creek bridge (920 feet). When snow is lacking here, drive on.

The Tour: Ski across the Miller River and enjoy the snow-covered "mushroom rocks" in the creekbed, then head into the forest to glide under the snow-laced trees. Rock walls to the side of the road are often decorated with streamers of ice. Views are few—Temple, Lennox, and Crosby Mountains enclose the valley on both sides. At 4 miles Goat Creek merges from the south and the Money Creek valley bends sharply northwest to enter a narrow gorge (1,900 feet) where the road begins to climb steeply. The road banks are near vertical here and subject to rock slides. After 5 miles the road makes a short switchback, and a break in the forest gives views of the snowy slopes on Lennox Mountain. At 6½ miles find Lake Elizabeth on the right side of the road (2,850 feet). The road continues on for ¼ mile to a narrow pass overlooking the Tolt Valley.

30 MILLER RIVER

Class: self-propelled
Rating: easiest
Round trip: 4–14 miles
Skiing time: 3 hours–2 days
Elevation gain: up to 2,100 feet

High point: 2,200 feet at road-end
Best: mid-December–January
Avalanche potential: low
Map: Green Trails, Skykomish No. 175

Moss-draped trees, rivers, waterfalls, and mountain goat viewing ensure an interesting tour on a motor-free route up the narrow Miller River valley. The tour follows a logging road through rain forest–like vegetation with looks up to 5,591-foot Cascade Mountain and Maloney Ridge. Backcountry skiers may continue on from the end of the road for a 1½-mile trail adventure to Lake Dorothy.

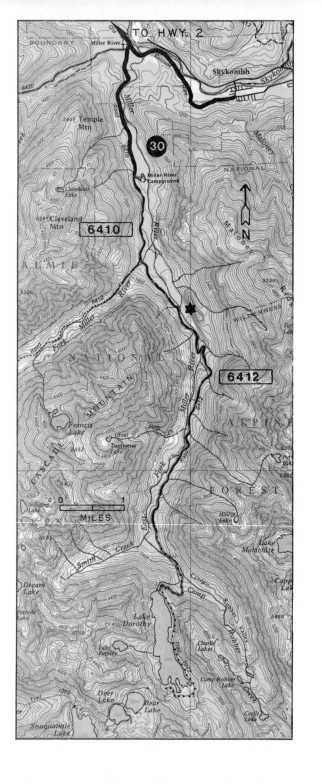

Lake Dorothy Trail after an early-season snow melt

Access: Drive Highway 2 to the Money Creek Campground sign (located at the entrance of the tunnel, 2.7 miles west of Skykomish). Turn south on the Old Cascade Highway for 1 mile then go right on Miller River Road No. 6410. After 200 feet Money Creek Road branches off on the right (see Tour 29). Continue straight for 2.1 miles to the end of the plowing at Miller River Campground (1,040 feet) or to the snowline. (The road is plowed on a low-priority basis, so always carry a shovel and tire chains.)

The Tour: From the parking area at the edge of the campground follow Miller River Road up-valley. Using the honor system rather than a gate, this road has been reserved for skiers, snowshoers, and hikers. Some car and truck drivers don't understand the honor system so do not be surprised if you have to ski around tire ruts for the first ½ mile or so.

The road heads through dense timber along the edge of the Miller River for 1½ miles. When the nearly overgrown West Fork Road branches off right, keep left and cross the West Fork Miller River (1,300 feet). Just ⅛ mile beyond the bridge a turnout on the left side of the road serves as the first of the two goat-viewing spots. Look across the valley and watch the cliffs for little snow patches that walk.

The second goat-viewing spot is the East Fork Miller River Bridge, which is crossed at 3 miles (1,450 feet). The road then makes its one and only switchback of the tour before heading on up the valley for another 2½ miles to reach the Lake Dorothy Trailhead at 5½ miles (2,100 feet).

If you have proper backcountry equipment and the skills required to ski up a narrow trail, head over to the far right end of the trailhead parking area. The climb is moderate for the first mile to the confluence of Camp Robber Creek and the Miller River (2,480 feet). Beyond the bridge, ski straight up into a basin then contour right traversing around the headwall to the crest. Once up top follow the route of the trail and climb steadily northwest to the lake outlet (3,058 feet).

---

31 EAGLE CREEK

Class: *multiple use*
Rating: *more difficult*
Round trip: *up to 10 miles*
Skiing time: *4 hours*
Elevation gain: *up to 3,100 feet*

High point: *4,000 feet*
Best: *mid-December–March*
Avalanche potential: *moderate*
Maps: *Green Trails, Skykomish No. 175 and Monte Cristo No. 143*

Eagle Creek is an easy-access area with miles of roads for touring, open hillsides for cross-country descents, and endless views for enjoying. The road system lies on the edge of the Eagle Rock Roadless Area and secluded campsites may be reached by continuing into the backcountry from the end of this tour.

Note: Avalanche hazard is very high in the Eagle Creek valley during and for several days after a rainstorm or wet snowfall. Also, use caution when visiting here on any unseasonably warm day, as the steep hillsides are prime candidates for spring sluffs.

Access: Drive Highway 2 to Skykomish. From the gas station, continue east 0.7 mile then go left on Beckler River Road No. 65 (880 feet). When snowfall has been heavy this is the starting point for skiing. If the road is drivable, and it usually is by February, continue on 0.8 mile to the first major intersection and go left on Road 6510. Skiing directions start here; hopefully you will be able to drive farther.

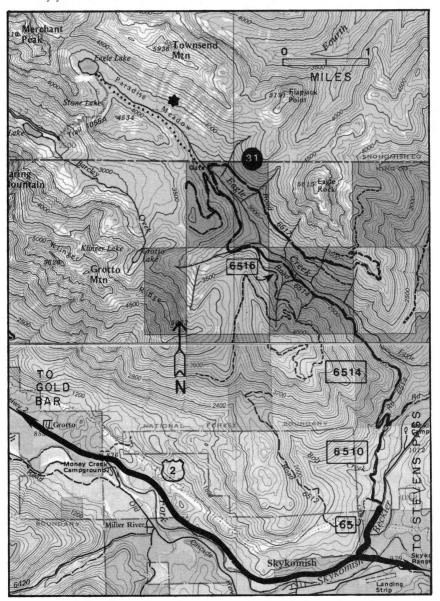

Eagle Creek and Beckler River valleys

The Tour: Ski Road 6510 up a short incline to a large intersection. Stay to the right and traverse north on the main road, tunneling through a dense canopy of forest and brush. At the end of the first mile the road divides again (1,200 feet). Go left on Road 6514.

Road 6514 climbs rapidly with a short series of steep switchbacks that are difficult to descend when icy. A viewpoint of Mounts Hinman and Daniels along this section helps to relieve the tedium of the steady ascent.

At 1¾ miles the road arrives at a large platform then turns northwest into the Eagle Creek drainage. When the snow is unstable, this is the safest turn-around point. Beyond, the beautiful Eagle Creek valley has been mercilessly logged from valley floor to ridge tops. Expect sliding when the snow is unstable, especially at the natural hillside drainage points.

Views increase as you head up the valley. Eagle Rock (5,615 feet) is the first peak to come into view, followed by the forested slopes of Flapjack Point and then the long, open summit of Townsend Mountain. At 3½ miles awaits a major junction. Continue straight ahead on Road 6514 (to the left, Road 6516 climbs up and over potentially avalanche-prone slopes to Klinger Ridge and excellent views).

At 4 miles cross a small creek with a view of Grotto Mountain. The road divides again at 4¾ miles. Go left, still on Road 6514, and switchback up. The road divides yet again in ¼ mile; go right to the ridge top and enjoy the views that start with the glacier-cut valley between Baring Mountain and

Merchant Peak, extend down Barclay Creek to the South Fork Skykomish River, and end in the pinkish haze of the Puget Sound Basin.

A backcountry tour to 3,888-foot Eagle Lake can be made from the end of Road 6514. Simply follow the ridge, skiing as close to the crest as possible for 2 miles to the lake. The steep slopes descending from Townsend Mountain are very avalanche-prone; if camping, pitch your tent at little Stone Lake.

The two small lakes between Flapjack Point and Townsend Mountain are another popular backcountry destination. Climbing skins are necessary for this trip. From the intersection at 4¾ miles, go right on Road 6517. Cross Eagle Creek and then leave the road and enter the forest, heading northeast towards a 4,680-foot saddle between Flapjack and Townsend. The first lake lies directly north of the saddle at 4,400 feet. The second lake is to the west on a small bench at 4,860 feet.

32 TONGA RIDGE AND FOSS RIVER

Tonga Ridge

Class: self-propelled
Rating: most difficult
Round trip: 5 miles
Skiing time: 3 hours
Elevation gain: 1,100 feet
High point: 4,800 feet
Best: November and April
Avalanche potential: moderate
Map: Green Trails, Skykomish No. 175

Foss River

Class: self-propelled
Rating: easiest
Round trip: 2–20 miles
Skiing time: 1 hour–2 days
Elevation gain: 100–2,960 feet
High point: 4,320 feet
Best: mid-December–April
Avalanche potential: low
Maps: Green Trails, Skykomish No. 175 and Stevens Pass No. 176

From the first snowfall of late autumn to those rocky last runs of early summer, there is skiing to be found in the Foss River area. Routes have a special scenic character, whether of moss-draped trees on the serene valley floor or of icy-craggy Cascade summits.

Access: Drive Highway 2 east 1.8 miles from Skykomish then turn right on Foss River Road No. 68. After 1.2 miles turn right again, still on Road 68. At 2.5 miles pass under a railroad trestle to find the winter parking area (1,280 feet).

Tonga Ridge: In early and late season the best skiing is on Tonga Ridge where numerous viewpoints of Mount Baring, Glacier Peak, and the ramparts leading to Mount Daniel offer a diversion from backcountry exploring. The

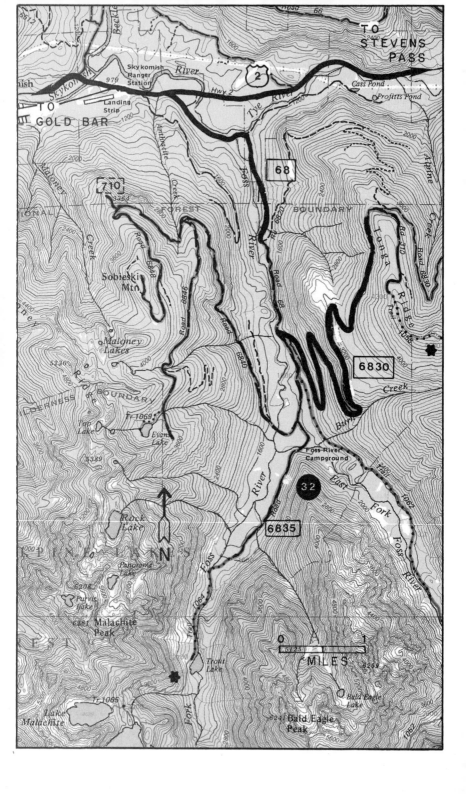

Snow-covered forest

route is not recommended in midwinter due to (1) snowmobilers and (2) avalanches which somehow fail to eliminate (1).

From the winter parking area drive up Foss River Road another 1.1 miles then turn left on Tonga Ridge Road No. 6830. Go uphill for 3.4 miles to the road's highest point (3,880 feet) and find Spur Road 310 on the right, signed "Tonga Ridge." Ski (or drive, as the case may be) 1.5 miles up the steep spur to its end at the trailhead (4,400 feet).

The trail begins by abruptly climbing, gaining 200 feet of elevation along the edge of a clearcut. Above the logged area head into the forest for a mile before breaking out into the meadows of the Alpine Lakes Wilderness. The ski route follows the upsy-downsy way of the summer trail and contours another 2 miles around Sawyer Mountain to Sawyer Pass (4,800 feet).

Foss River: Except for the first mile, Foss River Road is reserved for nonmotorized sports and most snowmobilers abide by the rule. The Forest Service additionally has marked two ski trails into the Alpine Lakes Wilderness. The road therefore can be heartily recommended for an afternoon or overnight tour during the loudest months of winter.

From the 1,280-foot parking area, ski the long mile to Tonga Ridge Road. At the junction go straight, still on Road 68.

At 2 miles the East Fork Foss River Trail is passed on the left. The first 5 miles of the trail makes a challenging backcountry tour through the forest. Just ½ mile beyond the East Fork Trailhead, Road 6835 branches to the left. Road 6835 ends at the West Fork Foss River Trailhead.

Continuing on Foss River Road No. 68, cross the West Fork Foss River Bridge at 2¾ miles, then start the long climb to Maloney Ridge. The bridge is a good turnaround point when conditions are unstable. At ¼-mile beyond the bridge a spur road branches off on the right and shortly after a spur road heads off to the left; stay on the main road for a long climbing traverse through forest and clearcuts.

A major intersection is reached at 6½ miles. Keep right, staying with Road 68 until Spur Road 710 branches off to the right at 8¾ miles. Follow the spur road for a final ¼ mile to the radio tower (3,364 feet). The views extend up and down the Skykomish River to Mount Index, Mount Baring, and Glacier Peak.

33 SKYLINE RIDGE

Class: self-propelled
Rating: backcountry
Round trip: 4 miles
Skiing time: 3 hours
Elevation gain: 1,200 feet

High point: 5,200 feet
Best: January–March
Avalanche potential: low
Maps: Green Trails, Stevens Pass No. 176
    and Bench Mark Mtn. No. 144

Years before skinny skis, refugees from the mobs at the Stevens Pass Ski Area were fleeing across the highway to untracked slopes of Skyline Ridge (formerly Heather Ridge). Though the long, south-facing ascent rarely offered the far-famed "Stevens powder," and explorers were burdened by heavy mountaineering outfits, they returned time and time again. Nowadays Skyline Ridge is an extremely popular tour for backcountry skiers. The reason is the same now as it was then—views over miles and miles of white-topped peaks and untracked slopes to sculpt turns.

Access: Drive Highway 2 to the summit of Stevens Pass and park on the north side of the road (4,050 feet).

The Tour: Follow the cat track up the hill passing several cabins tucked in the trees. Stay with the track as it angles across the ridge to a telephone relay station at the foot of the open slopes.

To the right of the telephone relay station, a primitive road, obscured by snow, heads steeply up. Climbing skins are very helpful. A quarter of the

Skyline Ridge

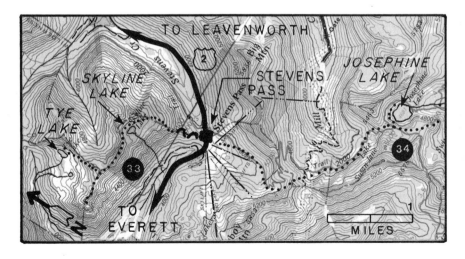

way to the ridge top the road fades away. Continue upward; in unstable conditions stay to the left (west) side of the open slope.

At 4,900 feet, the radio relay shed is passed and the hard climbing ends. Mount Hinman and Daniel come into view. However, the really big picture awaits above. Ski northwest just below the heavy timber, then turn uphill in thinning forest to the snowy plain that is Skyline Lake (5,092 feet). Continue to the base of a rock knob on the ridge crest. Unless equipped with ice ax, do not try for the top; be satisfied with the superb view from the saddle which includes Glacier Peak to the north and Mount Stuart to the southeast.

Warm up on the short slopes around Skyline Lake then head northwest. Ski north into the trees then over the edge of the ridge and telemark your way into some of the finest powder bowls around. The fun ends 1,300 feet below when you reach the Pacific Crest Trail (which may be invisible under the snow) or an obvious west-east–running drainage. At this point you should put on your climbing skins and climb back to Skyline Lake. Or, if you do not mind skiing across several very active avalanche chutes, the Pacific Crest Trail may be followed back to the parking lot.

34 JOSEPHINE LAKE

Class: *self-propelled*
Rating: *backcountry*
Round trip: *7 miles*
Skiing time: *4 hours*
Elevation gain: *1,500 feet*

High point: *5,300 feet*
Best: *January–February*
Avalanche potential: *high*
Map: *Green Trails, Stevens Pass*
   No. 176

See map on page 103

Excellent powder bowls and outstanding views turn this short tour to Josephine Lake into an all-day affair. You should plan an early start, not only to ensure enough time to ski all the bowls, but also to allow time to climb through the Stevens Pass Ski Area before the lifts open (that means before 9 A.M.).

The potential for avalanches on this tour is high, so ski to Josephine Lake only when the snow conditions are very stable and carry a full complement of backcountry equipment including shovels, avalanche beacons, climbing skins, and a good map.

Access: Drive Highway 2 to the summit of Stevens Pass and park at the ski area (4,050 feet).

Opposite: *Scenery along the Josephine Lake ski route*

The Tour: Walk up to the ski area and stay to the left, passing around the front of the day lodge. Ski south through the downhill area staying as close as possible to the base of the steep hills. Keep out of the way of out-of-control downhill skiers on these beginner and intermediate runs. At the upper end of the basin, pass the Tye Mill chairlift and continue straight until your way is blocked by a nearly vertical hill. Go left and head up the right-hand side of a well-groomed ski run.

At the top of the ridge (5,200 feet), ski to the right then head down the east side, descending either through the trees or on the groomed slope. The slope, groomed or ungroomed, drops to the upper end of Mill Creek (5,000 feet). Locate the powerlines, and continue down to the 4,800-foot level. If you are still on the groomed slopes now is the time to leave them; go to the right, skiing on an easterly course into the trees.

You should be on a sloping bench which is followed east. Stay well below the cliffs on the right. Use the protective cover of the trees when possible. (The north-facing slopes between the cliffs and trees are avalanche-prone and extremely hazardous after any heavy snowfall or when warmed by the spring sun.) Despite all precautions, a couple of hazardous chutes are traversed. These are easy to pick out; the trees on them never grow more than 10 feet tall.

Near the end of the sloping bench is a thick band of trees. Using them for cover, climb the steep hillside to tiny Lake Susan Jane (4,640 feet). Ski around the north side of the lake and at the far (east) end head up the right-hand side of an open slope. At the upper end of the slope follow a stream-cut gully through the trees to a small open bench (4,900 feet). Ski across the bench, then climb left to an upper bench overlooking Josephine Lake. Stop well before the edge of the trees; a band of cliffs lies between you and the lake. Plan to enjoy a long lunch here, gazing over the lake to the southeast where the snow-covered Bulls Tooth overshadows its neighbors.

To reach the lake, ski left through the trees until you are beyond the cliffs, then descend 400 feet to the lake. When the snow is good be sure to save enough time to ski the open bowls above the lake.

Snow doughnuts

35 SMITH BROOK AND LAKE VALHALLA

Smith Brook

Class: multiple use
Rating: more difficult
Round trip: 4 miles
Skiing time: 2 hours
Elevation gain: 800 feet
High point: 4,000 feet
Best: January–March
Avalanche potential: high
Map: Green Trails, Bench Mark
   Mtn. No. 144

Lake Valhalla

Class: partially self-propelled
Rating: backcountry
Round trip: 7½ miles
Skiing time: 4 hours
Elevation gain: 1,900 feet
High point: 5,100 feet
Best: January–March
Avalanche potential: high
Map: Green Trails, Bench Mark
   Mtn. No. 144

Smith Brook is unique. This moderately high-elevation tour has snow all winter and is always a safe bet when the snow is chancy at lower elevations. The gradually climbing road makes for easy touring, ideal for beginners and family groups. Best of all, neither Sno-Park permit nor trail pass is needed to ski here.

Since the Forest Service turned over the entire Mill Creek Sno-Park to commercial interests many skiers have turned to Smith Brook Road as an alternative. However, Smith Brook is definitely not the cross-country skiers' paradise that Mill Creek was. Parking is the first challenge encountered. The only legal parking is ⅛ mile east of Smith Brook Road. From the parking area skiers

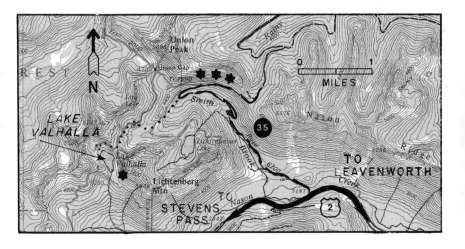

View over snow-covered Lake Valhalla

must either walk along Highway 2 or ski the gravel-studded road bank. No matter which way you go, you will have to claw your way up a wall of snow which can be 10 to 15 feet high. Probably the worst feature of this tour is the extreme avalanche danger beyond the 2-mile point. Unless you are backcountry-equipped and have a sound understanding of avalanche hazards, you must be satisfied with a short tour.

Smith Brook: Smith Brook Road lies 4.7 miles east of Stevens Pass on a divided section of Highway 2. If approaching from the west it is necessary to drive 6 miles beyond Stevens Pass to the Mill Creek U-turn. Head back west towards the pass 1.2 miles to find the parking area (3,200 feet). *Note:* Improperly parked cars will be towed. Properly parked cars are also occasionally towed. Until the situation has been clarified with a sign explaining how to park, do not leave your car here overnight.

Lake Valhalla: Walk up Highway 2 for ⅛ mile or, if the snow is clean, ski the road bank. Once on Smith Brook Road begin a gentle climb through alternating forest and clearcuts. At 1¾ miles the road makes a broad switchback in a large clearcut before reentering the trees. This is the turn-around point for those skiers who are not heading on to Lake Valhalla.

Backcountry skiers continuing on to Lake Valhalla should ski up the road for about 2 miles. Leave the road at the corner of a switchback and continue straight into a meadow (4,000 feet).

About 400 to 500 feet beyond the meadow, turn left and ski to the hillside then climb to the right over rolling slopes. At about 4,500 feet the forest cover thins. Ahead is an avalanche-prone hillside on the flank of avalanche-prone Lichtenberg Mountain; swing to the right and continue climbing to an open bowl.

Looking straight ahead, southwest, is a saddle. That is the goal. Ski to the northwest, then head southwest for a climbing traverse across a hillside cut by deep gullies. The 5,100-foot saddle is reached at 3½ miles from Highway 2.

Lake Valhalla lies 400 feet below the saddle. To ski the lake, head down to the right; slopes to the left could slide. If the climb back out from the lake is too intimidating, try heading up to the top of the 5,700-foot knob above the saddle for some exhilarating skiing down lightly timbered slopes.

---

36 JIM HILL

Lanham Lake

Class: self-propelled
Rating: backcountry
Round trip: 3½ miles
Skiing time: 4 hours
Elevation gain: 1,283 feet
High point: 4,143 feet
Best: December–March
Avalanche potential: none
Map: Green Trails, Bench Mark
    Mtn. No. 144

Jim Hill

Class: self-propelled
Rating: mountaineer
Round trip: 8 miles
Skiing time: 6 hours
Elevation gain: 3,805 feet
High point: 6,200 feet
Best: February–May
Avalanche potential: moderate
Maps: USGS, Labyrinth Mountain,
    Stevens Pass, Mount Howard, and
    Chiwaukum Mountains

Two destinations, a beautiful subalpine lake and a scenic mountain top, make this one of the classic backcountry skiing areas in the Cascades. Lanham Lake, a short but rather difficult tour, is an excellent midwinter destination. Jim Hill is at its best in the spring after the snow stabilizes. Once you have pieced the maps together, Jim Hill is likely to become an annual event for all telemark enthusiasts.

Both trips require a covering of at least 3 feet of snow to be fun. Heavy brush makes skiing nearly impossible when snow cover is insufficient.

Access: Drive Highway 2 east 5.8 miles beyond Stevens Pass to Mill Creek Road (2,800 feet); a U-turn road gives access for westbound traffic. The large parking area here is for the Stevens Pass Nordic Center. This is a groomed area and a fee is charged to use the trails on days when the center is open. Park in the outer lot, the inner parking area is blocked off after 4 P.M.

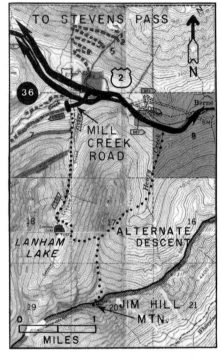

Lanham Lake: Backcountry skiers are allowed up the first 30 feet of the groomed Mill Creek Road without buying a pass. You must leave the road at the Lanham Lake Trailhead and head up the steep hillside on the narrow trail. Many skiers walk the first section. You are not allowed to use the roads, which provide easier access to the powerlines without buying a trail pass *when the center is open*. When the center is closed, ski up Mill Creek Road for about 1 mile then follow a route that currently goes by the name of Chuga Chuga. This groomed trail climbs up and to the east intersecting the Lanham Lake Trail under the powerlines at the edge of the dropoff overlooking Lanham Creek. Go right and head uphill into the trees. The trail parallels Lanham Creek through alternating forest and old clearcuts and across several old logging roads. Keep left, staying approximately 500 feet from the creek.

As the valley narrows, continue straight ahead on a climbing traverse above the creek. A scant ½ mile of steep climbing leads to Lanham Lake (4,143 feet). Nestled in the trees, this serenely frozen lake offers many fine picnic and campsites with views up to the icicled ramparts of Jim Hill Mountain.

Jim Hill: Ski to Lanham Lake, then head east, across the outlet. When you reach the hillside, begin a climbing traverse south. Find a shelf and follow

Lanham Lake and Jim Hill Mountain

it back to the northeast to the 5,650-foot saddle on the crest of a very narrow ridge.

Climb south along the crest of the ridge until it divides at 6,200 feet then ski up a small basin. Continue up to a small dip on the summit. This is an avalanche-prone area so be sure the snow is stable before making the final ascent.

For the descent, head back down the way you came as far as the saddle. The safest, least avalanche-prone route is the ridge crest. Watch for cornices and unstable snow. From the 5,650-foot saddle you have two choices for descending. You may follow your ascent route back or drop down the Henry Creek drainage (recommended). Stay to the west of Henry Creek. You should intersect Highway 2 no more then 1½ miles below Mill Creek Road. Hitchhike or walk up the road to return to the start.

37 CHIWAUKUM MOUNTAINS (SCOTTISH LAKES)

Coulter Ski Trail

Class: self-propelled
Rating: most difficult
Round trip: 13 miles
Skiing time: 6 hours
Elevation gain: 2,800 feet
High point: 5,000 feet
Best: January–February
Avalanche potential: low
Maps: Green Trails, Wenatchee Lake
　　No. 145 and Chiwaukum
　　Mtns. No. 177

Scottish Lakes

Class: self-propelled
Rating: backcountry
Round trip: over 20 miles
Skiing time: 1–4 days
Elevation gain: 100–2,000 feet
High point: 7,000 feet
Best: January–April
Avalanche potential: moderate
Maps: Green Trails, Wenatchee Lake
　　No. 145 and Chiwaukum
　　Mtns. No. 177

The Scottish Lakes area of the Chiwaukum Mountains is a perfect mixture of rolling hills, snow-covered alpine lakes, open meadows, forests, and outstanding views. Backcountry skiers have the option of carving turns on open slopes or through the trees. If the telemark turn has somehow eluded you, this country is equally good for touring. Best of all, the weather here tends to be just a little bit better than at Stevens Pass or Lake Wenatchee.

The Scottish Lakes area was first developed by Peg and Bill Stark. In addition to establishing the routes and trails to the lakes and braes, they established Nomad Camp with tent cabins and food service. In 1993 they retired and in 1995 the camp reopened under the management of High Country Adventures, Inc., P.O. Box 2023, Snohomish, WA 98291-2023.

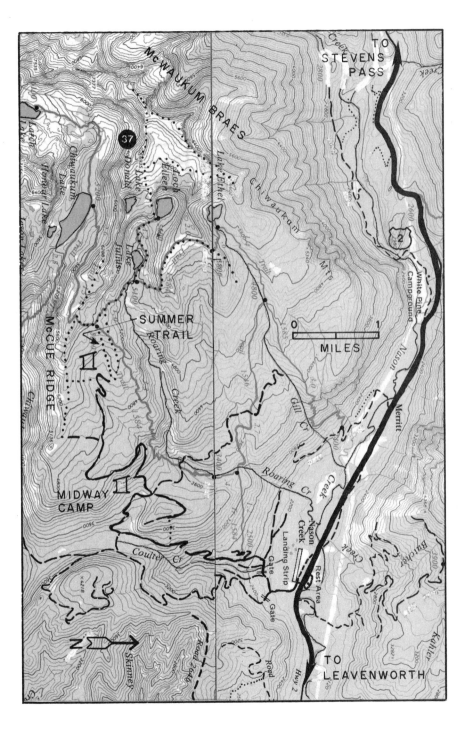

Lake Julius below the McWaukum Braes

Although the Scottish Lakes are in the Alpine Lake Wilderness and open to everyone, visitors who attempt to completely disassociate themselves from the concession are plagued with access problems. The trailhead is on private land and parking is non-existent. Independent visitors must be prepared to park either at one of the Lake Wenatchee Sno-Parks or in Leavenworth and hitchhike back to the start. Under current management, parking comes with the price of having your packs or yourself carried by Sno-Cat to the wilderness boundary (a good deal) where the independent-minded could head out to camp in a secluded spot.

The Coulter Ski Trail is the best route to use if you decide to ski into the Scottish Lakes. The trail involves considerable climbing through old clearcuts, is moderately scenic, and requires a large expenditure of energy. Skiing is at its best when there is a minimum of 2 feet of snow at the parking area.

Access: Drive Highway 2 east 17 miles from Stevens Pass. Just opposite the closed Rest Area turn right onto the Coulter Creek road system (2,200 feet). Park in the area reserved for camp patrons.

Coulter Ski Trail: Starting from the railroad tracks, walk the roughly plowed road for the first ¼ mile to a signed junction and turn right on the

114

Coulter Ski Trail. Another ¼ mile brings a left turn at a large Y (2,300 feet). As the way climbs, stay left at the next intersection then go right at the two following intersections. At 1¾ miles enter the base of a clearcut. Ascend to the left, avoiding the cliffs. After gaining 200 feet, head up the clearcut, aiming for the upper right side. Crest the ridge at 3,900 feet to find a road and tremendous views of the Chiwaukums and Nason Ridge. Bear left, losing a few hundred feet, to a three-way intersection at 3 miles.

Turn up, following the cat tracks past Midway Camp and marked ski trails. At 6½ miles is Nomad Camp (5,000 feet) and the end of the Coulter Ski Trail. Either stay at Nomad Camp or follow the ridge toward Lake Julius and choose from among the numerous campsites along the ridge, the Roaring Creek valley below, or at Loch Eileen.

Scottish Lakes: The Starks laid out and marked a number of trails beginning at Nomad Camp for all degrees of skill and energy. Serious backcountry skiers will be unable to resist the formidable all-day trip up the McWaukum Braes. From the end of the Coulter Ski Trail follow the Summer Trail along the ridge above Roaring Creek for 1½ miles, then descend. Head east along the valley floor ½ mile to Lake Julius and pass it on the north. Shortly beyond the lake, the valley makes an abrupt turn to the north. Following the obvious drainage, climb 500 feet in 1 mile to Loch Eileen.

Above Loch Eileen, head east, climbing steeply. This short section has the only avalanche potential in the area and should not be crossed in unstable conditions. At the top of the narrow ledge, go right, skiing above 5,900-foot Lake Donald. From here, the skiing is open to the top of any of the three braes.

McCue Ridge is another excellent run. The trip through forest and meadows is marked for the whole 2½ miles of ridge crest and along several access trails. It can be skied in all weather conditions but is best on sunny days when views from a 6,258-foot crest extend for miles over the whole Chiwaukum Range.

Overlook of Coulter and Nason Creek valleys

38 WENATCHEE RIVER WAY

Class: *multiple use*
Rating: *easiest*
Round trip: *8 miles*
Skiing time: *4 hours*
Elevation gain: *413 feet*

High point: *2,000 feet*
Best: *January–February*
Avalanche potential: *low*
Map: *Green Trails, Leavenworth No. 178*

The Wenatchee River Way is a pastoral tour through forest and around farmer's fields to find winter's heartland along the snow-covered banks of the Wenatchee River. This is an easy tour, on a gated forested road, with only a few hills. The one major challenge involves crossing Chiwaukum Creek,

Skiing along the edge of the Wenatchee River on Wenatchee River Way

and unless you can ski on water, you will need to use the busy Highway 2 bridge. The happy result of this access problem is that few snowmobiles find their way here.

Access: Drive Highway 2 east 26.8 miles from Stevens Pass to the Tumwater Campground entrance. Park in the large turnout on the east side of the highway (1,687 feet).

The Tour: The trip begins with a tour through Tumwater Campground. Follow one of the north-heading loop roads and keep Highway 2 on your left as you ski past snow-covered campsites. After ½ mile, reach the northern end of the campground and a wall of brush. Ski left, up to the highway,

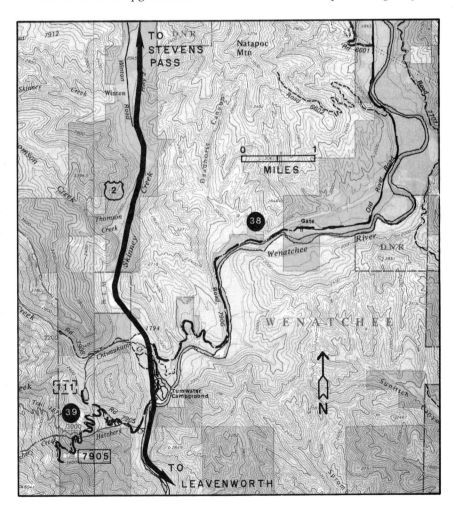

then walk across the Chiwaukum Creek Bridge. Get off the highway as soon as possible and ski along the edge until you intercept Wenatchee River Road.

Follow Wenatchee River Road as it heads to the right, crossing an open meadow. At the far side of the meadow the road bends to the left and heads uphill into the forest. Spur roads on the right lead to a future housing development. With more ups than downs, Wenatchee River Road climbs to a high point about 400 feet above the river at 1½ miles from Tumwater Campground. Pass a large sandstone outcropping before starting a lazy descent towards the river.

At 2 miles the road passes between a house and a barn, then reenters the woods. A ½ mile beyond you will reach the bank of the Wenatchee River. The road runs first north then east along the narrow band of land between the forested hillside and the river. Several small campsites are passed.

39 HATCHERY CREEK

Class: *multiple use*
Rating: *most difficult*
Round trip: *5 miles*
Skiing time: *3 hours*
Elevation gain: *1,100 feet*

High point: *2,800 feet*
Best: *mid-December–March*
Avalanche potential: *moderate*
Maps: *Green Trails, Leavenworth No. 178 and Chiwaukum Mtns. No. 177*

See map on page 117

Ski well-graded forest roads from the shady depths of Tumwater Canyon up to the sun-drenched outer slopes of the Chiwaukum Mountains. Views abound; from the ice-laced Wenatchee River to the snow and ice–plastered mountain tops.

Note: The upper section of the trip receives considerably more sunlight and warmth than the shady start. If you are waxing your skis be prepared for everything from powder snow to slush.

Access: Drive Highway 2 east 26.8 miles from Stevens Pass. Directly after passing the entrance to Tumwater Campground look for a wide turnout parking area on the right at the start of Hatchery Creek Road No. 7905 (1,687 feet). If you cross the Wenatchee River bridge you have gone too far.

The Tour: Ski the forest road along the river, passing several cottages before the uphill grind begins. At 1¼ miles, after a long series of switchbacks, reach an unmarked junction; stay right.

At 2 miles the road gains a 2,200-foot saddle between a rounded knob and the clearcut slopes of the main hill. At this point you have a choice. On the right, Spur Road 111 climbs gently for ½ mile to a small unnamed lake at 2,380 feet. Although views are few, this is a good destination and turnaround point. Skiers in search of expensive views should bypass the lake and continue the switchbacking ascent up sparsely wooded slopes. At 2¼ miles, stay right at another unmarked junction. Near 3 miles a spur road branches right to the Lake Augusta Trailhead parking area, an excellent protected campsite (2,800 feet), if you are looking for one.

The road continues on a short distance past the trailhead, then becomes a cat track, ending in steep clearcuts overlooking the Wenatchee River Valley and the rolling hills beyond. Avoid this upper road after winter storms as the steep logging clearings could slide.

Hatchery Creek Road

40 LAKE WENATCHEE STATE PARK

Class: groomed
Rating: easiest–most difficult
Round trip: up to 13 miles
Skiing time: 1–6 hours
Elevation gain: up to 430 feet

High point: 2,300 feet
Best: January–February
Avalanche potential: none
Map: Green Trails, Plain No. 146

If you have not skied the groomed trails at Lake Wenatchee State Park recently, it's time to revisit. The trail system has been expanded to include the Kahler Glen Golf Course, Nason Ridge (see Tour 41), and the northern section of the park. If you have never skied at the park, it is time for a first visit. Bring the whole family; the trails are wide, with lanes for diagonal striding and skating. The terrain is rolling, with trails to suit all tastes and abilities. The scenery is winter's finest: snow-covered forest, the ice-clogged Wenatchee River, and magnificent vistas over Lake Wenatchee.

Lake Wenatchee State Park keeps an area open for winter camping with a cooking shelter and, for the optimum of comfort, a heated bathroom. On

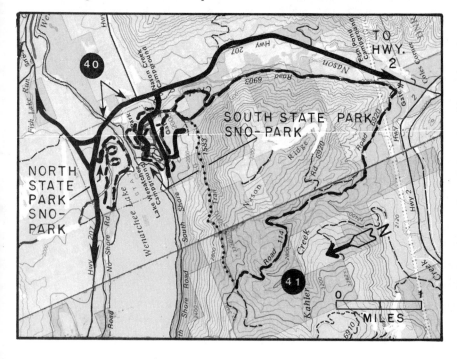

Lake Shore Loop

weekends, the park store sells snacks and warm drinks. A Sno-Park permit is required to park in one of the State Park's four parking sites (permits are sold at park store, weekends only). Three of the sites are located at the South Unit of the park. The fourth site is located at the North Unit. In 1996, Kahler Glen Golf Course was also offering Sno-Park parking (this parking was on a trial basis, so watch for future developments).

Access: Drive Highway 2 east 19 miles from Stevens Pass and at Coles Corner turn left on Highway 207 for 3.6 miles. Turn left again at the "South Entrance Lake Wenatchee State Park" sign. Cross Nason Creek, then stay right as the road splits and park in one of the three parking areas (1,900 feet). To reach Kahler Glen Golf Course, stay left when the road splits for 0.3 mile then go left for 0.4 mile to the Sno-Park. The north entrance State Park Sno-Park is located 1 mile north on Highway 207.

The Tour: Take time to study the signboard and map before you start. There are loops within loops throughout the park area. Loops average between 1 and 2 km in length (¾ and 1¼ miles). Connect a couple of these short loops and you will quickly create a 4- to 6-mile-long tour. The Lake Shore Loop takes you right along the edge of the lake where Poe and Nason Ridges and Dirtyface Peak reflect in the crystalline waters. The River View Loop heads over to the Wenatchee River and the Camp Loop runs through the campground. For a longer trip try the Nason Creek Loop and head over to the Kahler Glen Golf Course.

The golf course offers the opportunity to escape from the trees for a while. The open terrain is fun and scenic. Younger skiers seem to enjoy swooshing-tumbling runs off the landscaped hills.

The north section of the park has several short loops through the campground as well as a 2-mile loop that runs along the lakeshore. If you choose to ski to the lake, start your tour by heading left and avoid a dramatically steep descent.

---

41 LAKE VIEW TRAIL

Class: *groomed*
Rating: *more difficult*
Round trip: *16 miles*
Skiing time: *7 hours*
Elevation gain: *1,360 feet*

High point: *3,240 feet*
Best: *January–February*
Avalanche potential: *low*
Maps: *Green Trails, Plain No. 146*
and Lake Wenatchee No. 145

See map on page 120

Skating the golf course

In the expansive Lake Wenatchee snowmobile area, the Lake View Trail is the closest you will get to a backcountry experience. Although the trail is groomed with tracks for diagonal striding and a wide lane for skating, you will feel quiet isolated on the rarely visited lower reaches of Nason Ridge.

This is a long trail, but the groomed tracks and easy terrain make the ridgecrest viewpoint well within reach for many skiers. If the trail turns out to be too long, numerous satisfying, alternate turnaround points can be found along the route.

Note: Trail grooming is generally done for the weekends only. Mid-week visitors may find themselves breaking trail. Because the tour has a relatively low elevation start, snow quantity and quality vary from year

122

to year. Some years snowfall is insufficient for grooming. Call the State Park or Lake Wenatchee Forest Service office for current conditions.

Access: From Stevens Pass, drive east 19 miles to Coles Corner. Go left on Highway 207 for 3.6 miles then head left at the "South Entrance to Lake Wenatchee State Park" sign and cross Nason Creek. Continue on until the road divides. Go left for 0.3 mile then left again for 0.4 mile to the Kahler Glen Golf Course Sno-Park parking.

Note: Although the golf course is the best place to start this tour, the fate of this Sno-Park is uncertain. If you reach the golf course and do not see the public parking signs, return to the State Park and park in the first of the three Sno-Park lots.

The Tour: If starting from the golf course follow the trail that heads south, up the open hill from the parking area. Stay right at all intersections until the trail turns into a road that traverses the hillside overlooking the golf course. Stay with this road, passing intersections with the groomed golf course loops as well as a logging road that branches off on the right.

If starting from the State Park check the map board for the shortest route to the golf course. This involves crossing the park entrance road as well as South Shore Road then following the Nason Creek Loop to the golf course.

Lake View Trail

When convenient, cross to the west side of the golf course then climb the hill to meet the groomed Lake View Trail.

Once past the golf course, the groomed trail enters the forest, climbing very gradually as it heads south. Cross several open areas, burnt in the fires of 1994 and salvage-logged the following summer. Watch to the left for occasional glimpses of farms and Nason Creek below. At 2 miles from the golf course parking area the trail begins a gradual descent which ends ½ mile later at an old intersection. Go right on Road 6920 and begin the long and very gradual ascent up the south side of Nason Ridge. The trail follows the undulations of the terrain as it meanders across the clearcut hillside. At 3½ miles leave Road 6920 and go left on Spur Road 114. Like all intersections on this tour, the route is obvious if you follow the tracks of the groomer.

The trail heads up the Kahler Creek drainage. To the south, the Chiwaukum Mountains look very impressive under a winter coat. Near the 7½-mile point the trail steepens and the final ½ mile to the ridge crest holds promise of a swift descent. Once at the viewpoint gaze north to Pole Ridge and snow-smeared Dirtyface Peak. If you crane your neck and look around the trees, you may even see Lake Wenatchee below.

Looking at the map you will note that the Round Mountain Trail makes a tempting connection between the viewpoint and the golf course parking area. Do not be seduced by the short little line on the map unless you are good at skiing down steep, thickly forested slopes on narrow trail.

LAKE WENATCHEE

42 CHIWAWA SNO-PARK

Class: *groomed*
Rating: *easiest–most difficult*
Round trip: *up to 15 miles*
Skiing time: *2–8 hours*
Elevation gain: *up to 680 feet*

High point: *2,590 feet*
Best: *January–February*
Avalanche potential: *none*
Map: *Green Trails, Plain No. 146*

The three "skier only" loops at the Chiwawa Sno-Park are each distinctive and unique with ratings ranging from *easiest* to *most difficult*. Scenery varies from open forest where you may parallel a set of coyote tracks, to an ice-covered fantasy land along the banks of the Wenatchee River, to ridge-top views over the Wenatchee River and the broad Plain Valley.

Access: Drive Highway 2 east 19 miles from Stevens Pass then turn left on Highway 207 at Coles Corner and follow it for 4.6 miles. Cross the Wenatchee River, then go right at a Y on Chiwawa Loop Road for 1.5 miles to the Chiwawa Sno-Park (1,970 feet).

View of the Wenatchee River from the See and Ski Trail

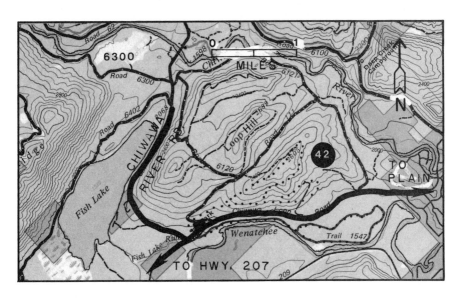

The Tour: A large information board and map at the parking lot help to orient the skier around the ski trails (three) and the snowmobile trails (endless).

Squirrel Run Trail is a 4-mile round trip and the *easiest* of the three trails to ski. The trail starts from the southwest corner of the Sno-Park and climbs gradually on a wide logging road. After ¼ mile cross a groomed snowmobile trail. At the ½-mile point cross a second snowmobile trail and then head steeply up on a narrow trail, leaving the machines behind. At ¾ mile the Flying Loop Trail branches off to the left and Squirrel Run levels off for a gently rolling traverse through the forest. The trail starts a ½-mile loop at 1¾ miles that gradually turns you back the way you came.

The *See and Ski Trail* starts across the road from the Sno-Park. This 6-mile route receives weekly grooming when there is enough snow. It is also the most scenic of the three trails. Ski through the forest for 1½ miles, then start a loop that sweeps along the edge of the Wenatchee River before heading back to the start on a series of abandoned logging roads. When the snow is soft this is an excellent tour for skiers of all abilities. When icy, only skiers who are comfortable with *more difficult* trails should attempt it.

The *Flying Loop* (named for the most common mode of descent) is the most challenging of the three trails. The first ¾ mile of the loop is skied in conjunction with the Squirrel Run Trail. Once the two trails part there is a 1½-mile climb to the ridge top, where you ski ½ mile along the forested crest before plunging back down. The final mile of the loop is a steep descent back to the Squirrel Run Trail. When the snow is soft, this 5-mile trail is skiable by anyone who has the skills required for skiing *most difficult* trails. When the snow is icy, skip this loop entirely.

LAKE WENATCHEE

43 LITTLE WENATCHEE RIVER ROAD

Class: multiple use
Rating: easiest
Round trip: 5 miles
Skiing time: 2 hours
Elevation gain: none

High point: 1,960 feet
Best: January–February
Avalanche potential: none
Map: Green Trails, Wenatchee Lake
 No. 145

Little Wenatchee River Road has ideal terrain for first-time skiers and family groups. The road is virtually flat, which will please the novices, and it is scenic, which will please everyone. A small meadow right at the start is a perfect place to take those first wobbly strides and nearby are small hills, ideal for children to zoom down with cries of "Watch me!"

Note: This is a low-elevation tour. When snowfall is light the road may be opened to winter logging. Call the Lake Wenatchee Ranger Station for updates on the most current snow and road conditions before heading out.

Access: Drive Highway 2 east 19 miles from Stevens Pass then turn left at Coles Corner on Highway 207. Head north then west around Lake Wenatchee for 10.9 miles. At the north end of the lake go left on Little Wenatchee River Road No. 6500 and drive 1½ miles to a gate. Park in the space provided (1,960 feet).

The Tour: Before heading out on your tour, use the meadow on the south side of the road for a few practice strides, glides, and stops. When you feel that everyone is balanced on their skis, start up the road.

Little Wenatchee River Road

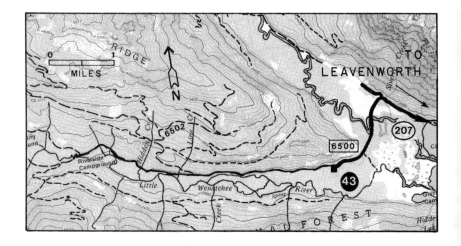

Little Wenatchee River Road tunnels through the forest along the base of Wenatchee Ridge. At the end of the first mile the river swings over to the north side of the valley and parallels the road. Views expand over the open river channel to Nason Ridge and Mount Mastiff.

The river swings back to the south side of the valley near 2¼ miles, and ¼ mile beyond Spur Road 6502 branches off to the right, marking a good turnaround point for groups with novice skiers.

Skiers continuing on will find that Little Wenatchee River Road remains nearly level until it divides at 4½ miles. Go left at this junction to reach Riverside Campground in ⅛ mile.

44 LEAVENWORTH

Class: groomed
Rating: easiest
Round trip: 9 miles of groomed trails
Skiing time: 1–2 days
Elevation gain: 200 feet

High point: 1,500 feet
Best: January–February
Avalanche potential: none
Map: Green Trails, Leavenworth No. 178

Ski immaculately groomed tracks along banks of the Wenatchee River, or roller-coaster up and down through ponderosa pine forest at the base of Tumwater Mountain. Enjoy first rate scenery then ski right to the edge of town for hot lunch before heading back out for the afternoon. If you like your

Ned Kuch Loop on Icicle River Trail

skiing mixed with all the amenities of life, then Leavenworth is the ideal winter destination.

An active cross-country ski club in Leavenworth keeps three trails groomed; a moderate fee is charged to help keep the grooming machines running.

Note: Leavenworth lies at the relatively low elevation of 1,200 feet. Insufficient snowfall can be a problem. If uncertain about snow conditions, inquire at the Leavenworth Ranger Station for the most current conditions.

Golf Course: Three areas are groomed near the city of Leavenworth. The most popular is the golf course. At the western end of town go south off Highway 2 on Icicle Road. Drive 0.6 mile to Golf Course Road then turn left for 0.1 mile.

The 12 km (7½ miles) of trails cruise over rolling terrain with excellent views of the surrounding mountains and the Wenatchee River. There are two main loops: Lazy River Trail, rated *easiest*, circles the golf course in about 2 miles, and Tumwater Loop, rated *more difficult*, is 1 mile longer and requires

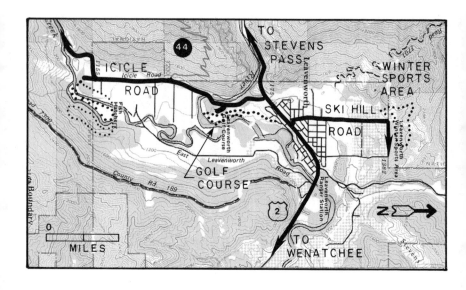

good control to avoid embarrassing yourself on the descents. From the golf course you may ski to Leavenworth on the Waterfront Park Trail for a quick meal at a downtown restaurant.

Icicle River Trail: Drive south from Highway 2 on Icicle Road for 2.6 miles. Leave the main road when it takes a 90-degree bend and go straight on CYO Road. Take the first left to find a large parking area and ticket booth.

The Icicle River Trail is made up of two loops, each approximately 4 km (2½ miles) long. The Ned Kuch Loop tours the nearly level ground between the parking area and the irrigation canal. The Meadow Loop is located on an island between the canal and Icicle River and has several interesting hills to navigate.

Leavenworth Ski Hill: Near the west end of town turn north on Ski Hill Road. Drive for 1.5 miles

Snow groomer

130

through orchards to the winter sports area. Just inside the gate is the start of a 2-km (1¼-mile) loop which is lighted at night. A second 3-km (2-mile) loop climbs to a viewpoint and is the most challenging in the Leavenworth Trail system.

45 ICICLE ROAD

Class: *multiple use*
Rating: *easiest*
Round trip: *9 miles*
Skiing time: *4 hours*
Elevation gain: *780 feet*

High point: *2,080 feet*
Best: *January–mid-March*
Avalanche potential: *low*
Maps: *Green Trails, Leavenworth No. 178 and Chiwaukum Mtns. No. 177*

A narrow valley, flanked by stunning mountains and sliced by a rushing creek that lives up to its icy name, is the objective of this extremely scenic tour up Icicle Creek valley.

Icicle Creek valley is very narrow and the surrounding mountains very steep. In midwinter, these two factors combine to keep the valley floor shaded and cool; a place where the snow lingers after it has melted from the groomed trails in the Leavenworth resort area (Tour 44).

A trail pass is not required to ski Icicle Road; however, your Sno-Park permit must be prominently displayed on your windshield.

Access: Drive Highway 2 to the western end of Leavenworth then turn south on Icicle Road. After 4 miles the road ends at a gate. The large Snow Lakes Trailhead does winter service as a Sno-Park.

Icicle Creek

The Tour: The first thing you will notice as you start up the valley is the scenery, from the serrated mountain tops thousands of feet above to the enchanting snow mushrooms covering the rocks in the river below. The next thing to notice is the presence or absence of the snowmobiles that are usually parked in a neat row just inside the gate. These snowmobiles belong to the families who live up the valley. The presence, or absence, of the snowmobiles should serve as a reminder that you are sharing your road with other users. Be on the lookout for machines at all times; however, these local commuters are some of the most polite and conscientious snowmobilers around so do not be afraid to take the kids with you.

From the moment you leave the car, the scenery is a distraction. Do not be tempted to leave the road in search of a better view of the creek—walls of snow overhang the river and are dangerous. The Eightmile Campground access road offers the first safe opportunity for some exploration along the edge of Icicle Creek.

At 4½ miles go left to Bridge Creek Campground (2,080 feet). This sparsely forested camp area makes an excellent lunch spot and turnaround point. Bridge Creek also marks the end of most snowmobile travel. If you wish to continue up-valley, you will probably have to break trail.

LEAVENWORTH
46 LAKE STUART

Class: *self-propelled*
Rating: *mountaineer*
Round trip: *up to 17 miles*
Skiing time: *2 days*
Elevation gain: *up to 3,064 feet*

High point: *5,064 feet*
Best: *April–mid-May*
Avalanche potential: *high*
Maps: *Green Trails, Chiwaukum Mtns.*
No. 177 and Mount Stuart No. 209

Nestled under the imposing north face of Mount Stuart, Lake Stuart is a tremendously scenic and very challenging backcountry ski trip, with, if the timing is right, tremendous skiing. This is a mountaineering tour, not because the skiing is difficult, but because competent map-reading skills and ability to accurately access avalanche conditions are requirements.

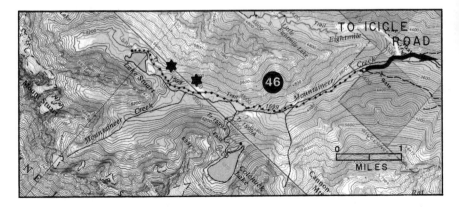

Lake Stuart and Mount Stuart

April, when the road is open to within a couple of miles of the trailhead, is generally the best time. If uncertain about road conditions, check with the Forest Service office in Leavenworth before heading out. You will need a wilderness permit for all day and overnight tours.

Access: Drive Highway 2 to Leavenworth. At the west end of town turn south on Icicle Road. At 8.5 miles go left on Road 7601, pass through Bridge Creek Campground, and cross Icicle Creek (2,000 feet). Tour mileages are noted from the bridge; any extra distance driven is a bonus.

The Tour: Ski or hike up Road 7601, passing the Eightmile Trail at 3 miles to reach the Mountaineer Creek Trailhead at an abrupt bend in the road at 4 miles (3,540 feet).

The trail starts by tunneling through thick timber along the edge of Mountaineer Creek. The confining wall of trees makes the trail easy to follow. Before long you will enter the Alpine Lakes Wilderness. Near the ¾-mile point the trail cuts across a steep slope with a direct drop to the creek. Avoid this short section by climbing to the terrace above then return to the trail once the danger is passed. Five miles from Icicle Road cross Mountaineer Creek on a broad bridge (3,920 feet). Use considerable caution here—no guardrails to keep the careless from a cold bath.

The next mile is spent climbing steeply, with an occasional switchback, past giant boulders and over rock shelves. Expect to walk in this section if the snowmelt is well advanced and do not be surprised if you lose the trail at any time. At 6½ miles from Icicle Creek, reach the Colchuck Lake intersection where the trail divides (4,600 feet). Follow the right fork into a broad valley. Use caution—in the next mile the route crosses the base of several avalanche chutes.

In the final mile to the lake the trail veers west, away from Mountaineer Creek, into the Lake Stuart drainage. Switchback up a steep hillside, then follow a narrow band of timber, staying well to the right of the creek, to reach the 5,064-foot lake, 8½ miles from Icicle Creek. Set up camp in the protected forest near either the outlet or the inlet of the lake.

Beautiful telemarking slopes above the lake beckon. The least avalanche-prone and largest bowls are northwest towards Jack Ridge and Horseshoe and Jack Lakes.

47 CAMAS LAND

Class: *multiple use*	**High point:** *3,450 feet*
Rating: *easiest*	**Best:** *mid-December–February*
Round trip: *4 miles*	**Avalanche potential:** *low*
Skiing time: *2 hours*	**Map:** *Green Trails, Liberty No. 210*
Elevation gain: *550 feet*	

Meadows keynote this tour, which starts at Camas Land (a 2-mile-long meadow), then climbs past several smaller meadows and marshes before the trip ends at a breathtaking viewpoint.

Although this is a multiple-use area, it is generally considered a safe tour for beginners. The steep access road tends to weed out the less determined and experienced winter visitors, leaving only the snowmobilers with some snow savvy and conscientious riding habits. On weekdays you may even have the tour to yourself.

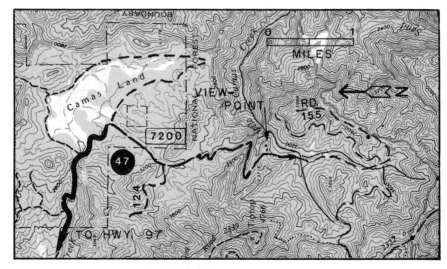

Access: Drive Highway 97 south 5.5 miles from Highway 2, then turn left (east) on Camas Creek Road No. 7200. If coming from the south, drive 16.2 miles north of Swauk Pass Summit. Once on Camas Creek Road, head up 2.2 miles to Camas Land, where the road divides. Stay right and follow the road as it skirts around the west side of the meadow for another 0.5 mile. The road takes you up a short, steep hill, before leveling off. Look for a parking place when the plowed road turns east (2,900 feet).

Note: The access road is plowed on a low-priority basis. Make sure the chains are in the car before heading out.

The Tour: Ski up Forest Road 7200 (Camas Creek Road), climbing gently along the east side of the open valley. On your right is a wide meadow, crisscrossed by small creeks, coyote trails, ski tracks, and snowmobile ruts.

Winter's delicate beauty

Horse Lake Mountain from viewpoint

Road 7200 is groomed for snowmobiles, so be ready to jump out of the way whenever a pack of machines zips by. However, for the most part this is a quiet tour as it passes from meadow into the forest. At ¾ mile pass Spur Road 124 on the right.

At 1½ miles Road 7200 levels off for ¼ mile, then climbs steeply over a shoulder of Tiptop Mountain to reach the viewpoint. Go left for the best views, being careful to stay well away from the overhung edge. Below is a series of weathered sandstone pinnacles and ribs. Beyond is a wall of strikingly beautiful white sandstone. To the east lies Burch Mountain, to the south are the Wenatchee Mountains, and to the west is the summit of Tiptop Mountain.

Miles of logging roads are waiting to be skied, if you care to continue on. Beyond the viewpoint Road 7200 makes two long descents, passing two meadows before ending at 3½ miles. The tour then continues on Spur Road 155, which climbs to the ridge tops and views.

48 KING CREEK ROAD

Class: *multiple use*
Rating: *most difficult*
Round trip: *8 miles*
Skiing time: *4 hours*
Elevation gain: *2,000 feet*

High point: *4,440 feet*
Best: *January–February*
Avalanche potential: *moderate*
Map: *Green Trails, Liberty No. 210*

Views, excellent powder bowls, and early-season corn snow all combine to make King Creek Road an outstanding tour. Although classified as multiple use, this road is too short to be of much interest to the motorized sled riders.

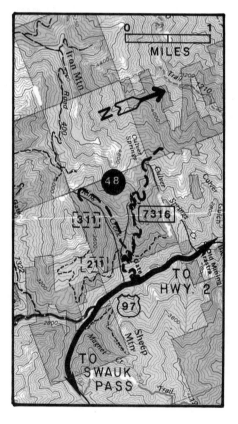

Access: Drive Highway 97 south 12.6 miles from Highway 2 or north from Swauk Pass for 9.5 miles. Park in the small plowed turnout on the west side of the highway at the start of King Creek Road No. 7316 (2,440 feet).

The Tour: King Creek Road starts off by following a section of the old Blewett Pass Road. Cross Peshastin Creek, pass a miner's cabin, then cross King Creek in the first ⅛ mile before beginning the real uphill grind with a switchback. At the second switchback you will be faced with a gate that must be climbed over or skied around. Beyond this point the road is poorly marked. Numerous minor spur roads branch off, generally unsigned. Near 2,800 feet, the first main spur road, No. 211, branches left.

Continue to climb the open,

The Stuart Range from King Creek Road

south-facing slope. If confused at intersections, the main road is always the one that switchbacks. Near 2¾ miles, the road swings into a small basin where Spur Road 311 branches to the left.

The road reaches a 3,843-foot vantage point at 3 miles. Below is Peshastin Creek and beyond Sheep Mountain, Tiptop Mountain, and Table Mountain can be seen. The road divides here. The right-hand fork offers an excellent launch pad down a powder bowl. The main road (No. 7316) follows the left spur for about 50 feet to a second intersection. Go right and continue on another mile to a ridge overlooking Negro Creek, the Three Brothers, and the Stuart Range.

49 FIVE MILE ROAD

Class: *self-propelled*
Rating: *more difficult*
Round trip: *6 miles*
Skiing time: *4 hours*
Elevation gain: *1,120 feet*

High point: *4,160 feet*
Best: *January–February*
Avalanche potential: *moderate*
Map: *Green Trails, Liberty No. 210*

Viewed from below, Tronsen Ridge seems to remain magically free of snow the entire winter. Whole hillsides on the west side of the ridge are snow-free the day after a storm. A tour up Five Mile Road offers an opportunity to check out this phenomenon, enjoy a day at this subtropical oasis, and, maybe, eat your lunch sitting on a dry log or rock instead of snow.

Access: Drive south on Highway 97 for 17.1 miles from Highway 2 or north from Swauk Pass for 5.2 miles and find a small parking area on the east side of the highway (3,040 feet). This parking area is plowed on a low-priority basis; after a heavy snowfall parking may not be available.

The Tour: Five Mile Road No. 7224 starts by heading south, paralleling Highway 97. After ⅛ mile the road swings east toward Tronsen Ridge and follows a creek into a large basin burned off during the dry summer of 1985. As the road enters the basin, it reaches the first of many unmarked junctions. Take the road to the far right, cross the creek, and climb around a narrow rib into a second basin. The road contours around this clearcut basin, crosses a second creek, and climbs a steep north-facing slope with a long switchback.

At 1¾ miles cross a creek then swing back toward the

The Stuart Range from Five Mile Road

burn, crossing an open, sunbaked slope. Snow may be thin along here so watch for rocks. At 2¾ miles, go right on Spur Road 311, which climbs directly to Tronsen Ridge for views of Iron Mountain and the rolling summits of the Wenatchee Mountains.

Skiers desiring more views may tackle one of the hills along the ridge. The 4,536-foot hill to the north can be approached without difficulty by following the ridge crest. The 4,970-foot hill to the south is best reached by branching right off Road 311 onto Spur Road 411. Ski to the end of the road, then go east, straight up to the top of the ridge. Follow the crest south to the summit ⅛ mile beyond.

50 TRONSEN MEADOW LOOPS

Class: *self-propelled*
Rating: *more difficult*
Round trip: *1–10 miles*
Skiing time: *3 hours–all day*
Elevation gain: *510 feet*

High point: *4,400 feet*
Best: *January–February*
Avalanche potential: *low*
Map: *Green Trails, Liberty No. 210*

Deep in the heart of Swauk Pass snowmobile country, the Forest Service has reserved an area for travelers powered solely by bread, cheese, energy bars, and enthusiasm. Although this area is not large, it is crisscrossed with so many trails that you can easily ski for an entire day without covering them all.

This is undoubtedly the best-developed nongroomed area set aside for

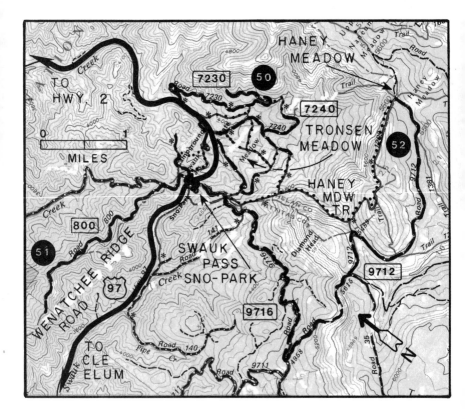

Skier crossing Tronsen Meadow

skiers in the northern half of the Washington Cascades. The Forest Service and local ski clubs deserve considerable approbation for the project, which includes marking of trails and the placement of numerous trail maps.

Access: Drive Highway 97 to the Tronsen Meadow Sno-Park located 0.8 mile north of the Swauk Pass summit (3,890 feet). Alternate Sno-Park parking is available at the Swauk Pass summit, Upper Tronsen Meadow Road, Tronsen Campground, and a couple of small turnouts near the summit.

The Tour: The loops in Tronsen Meadow and the trails around Swauk Pass are all candidates for *more difficult* or *most difficult* ratings. Some of the steeper trails might even be rated as most appropriate for *backcountry* equipped skiers. (If looking for an *easiest* tour, try a cruise around Tronsen Campground.)

The two main loops starting from the Tronsen Meadow Sno-Park are both *more difficult*. Check the map then ski up Road 7240 for a mile to a major intersection (4,160 feet). To ski the east loop, go left and continue the steady climb through forest with an occasional peek-a-boo view of the Stuart Range. At 1½ miles (4,400 feet) the road ends and the loop continues on trail for ½ mile. When you reach Road 7230 ski to the left and head back 1¾ miles. Just before reaching Highway 97 find a trail on your left which is followed back to Road 7240. Go right and return to the Sno-Park at 4¼ miles.

Equally enjoyable is the west loop around Tronsen Meadow. From the Sno-Park, ski 1 mile to the major junction then go to the right and follow the road/trail on a wide loop which cuts right across the top of Tronsen Meadow. At 2¼ miles go right on Road 7245 and descend toward Highway 97. Just before reaching the highway go right and ski the trail back to Road 7240.

For a little more challenge follow the marked trails across Tronsen Meadow then continue on the trail all the way to Road 9716. For a real challenge, no matter how good you think you are, head over Side-Step Hill. This trail leads to two meadows and can be truly thrilling when icy.

The Tronsen Meadow snowmobile closure area extends to the north side of the highway where several *most difficult* trails and routes can be found. The main access to this less developed area is from the Sno-Park on the north side of Swauk Pass Summit. Ski up Scotty Creek Road for 500 feet to the first corner then go straight, leaving snowmobile country for skier-only hills. Follow the old road 500 feet to an unmarked intersection where the road divides. If you go straight you will plunge down a broad, clearcut bowl. To the right is a ridge where, at a point of your own choosing, you can ski off the left side for a telemarking descent of the clearcut. For a looping traverse of a rounded knoll with twisted trees and views of the Stuart Range go left from the intersection and head down the overgrown road. When the road splits a second time, go left.

---

51 WENATCHEE RIDGE

Class: *mostly self-propelled*
Rating: *more difficult*
Round trip: *6 miles*
Skiing time: *4 hours*
Elevation gain: *458 feet*

High point: *4,560 feet*
Best: *January–February*
Avalanche potential: *low*
Map: *Green Trails, Liberty No. 210*

See map on page 142

Ridge after ridge, gleaming and snow-covered, roll south and north like white waves giving this top-of-the-world ski route along the clearcut crest of Wenatchee Ridge a sense of space and grandeur. And, if views are not

Snow-plastered trees along the Wenatchee River crest

enough of an incentive, the tour is fun for everyone from gung-ho five-year-olds to their telemarking parents.

Access: Drive Highway 97 to Swauk Pass (4,102 feet) and park in the northside Sno-Park. A large information board and map help skiers orient themselves before heading out on the maze of forest roads.

The Tour: Ski east from the information board on a groomed snowmobile route. Although most snowmobiles stay to the south side of the pass, expect to see a few in the first ½ mile. After 150 feet the road swings left (north). Ignoring the skiers' trail (Tour 50) which heads off to the right, follow the main road up the hillside. After skiing ½ mile reach a small saddle and junction (4,320 feet). Turn left on the snowmobileless Wenatchee Ridge Road (Scotty Creek Road descends straight ahead into snowmobile country).

Unlike other ski trails in the Swauk Pass area, the ridge road is mostly open (thanks to some energetic clearcutting). Views expand as you go. The road rolls, dropping from the ridge crest to contour around the higher peaks, then returning to the crest. Small knolls can be scenic lunch spots as well as fun ski hills. Backcountry-equipped skiers will find clearcut slopes of various steepness to challenge their turning abilities.

Just before the 3-mile point, the road splits. Climb the upper fork to the top of a small knoll for a final overlook of Red Top Mountain, the Swauk Valley, and the lowlands beyond.

---

52 HANEY MEADOW

Class: self-propelled
Rating: backcountry
Round trip: 10 miles
Skiing time: 8 hours
Elevation gain: 1,860 feet

High point: 5,960 feet
Best: January–February
Avalanche potential: moderate
Map: Green Trails, Liberty No. 210

See map on page 142

Excellent snow, surprising views, and great powder bowls make Haney Meadow a backcountry trip that is worth repeating. The meadow itself is a broad sloping plain, ringed by forested hills, but by no means the highlight of the tour. On weekends, the meadow is alive with snowmobiles and you may wish to stick to the skier-only areas.

Access: Drive Highway 97 to Swauk Pass and park in the Sno-Park on the south side of the road (4,102 feet).

The Tour: There are two ways to Haney Meadow. The easiest route follows groomed snowmobile roads for 10 comparatively gentle miles. Keep this option in mind in case you need to use it on the way back, that is, when the trail is ice hard or the snow pack is unstable.

The peaceful choice is the steep, narrow, challenging, but well-marked skier-only trail that reaches the meadow in 5 miles. From the upper end

Tronsen Ridge from Haney Meadow Trail

of the Sno-Park head uphill for ½ mile on a road shared with snowmobiles. The Haney Meadow Trail, marked only by a small metal sign on a tree at the turnoff, is the second trail branching off on the left-hand side of the road.

The trail starts with a climbing traverse across a wide clearcut followed by a short descent and more climbing. At 1½ miles (4,500 feet) a trail from Tronsen Meadow joins in on the left. The Haney Meadow Trail continues straight ahead, settling into the serious work of climbing a narrow valley on the east side of Diamond Head. Two avalanche chutes are crossed. If the snow pack is unstable (and it will be after most major snowfalls), detour off the trail and ski through the trees below.

The trail ascends around the head of the valley then climbs open slopes on the far side. A tall, lone tree near the top at 4 miles marks another intersection (5,840 feet). The trail to the right is an escape route to Table Mountain Road if the lower section of the Haney Meadow Trail is deemed unskiable on the way back. The Haney Meadow Trail continues straight ahead to the forest edge, then turns right to climb up and over an open knoll.

At 4½ miles the trail splits (5,960 feet); both forks lead to the meadow. Follow the left fork up to the ridge crest for a broad panorama of the Cascades; this is the proper turnaround for day tours. The right fork traverses around the ridge to rejoin the left. Once reunited, the way drops ½ mile to the end of an old spur road, which plunges down to Table Mountain Road. Turn right for the final, easy glide down to Haney Meadow (5,502 feet).

Are you camping? Include these in your day trips: Mount Lillian, Upper Naneum Meadows, the Mission Ridge Ski Area via Road 9712, and Lion Rock via Road 3500.

MISSION RIDGE

53 PIPELINE TRAIL

Class: groomed
Rating: more difficult
Round trip: 5 miles
Skiing time: 2 hours
Elevation gain: 370 feet

High point: 4,920 feet
Best: January–February
Avalanche potential: moderate at
   west end
Map: USGS, Mission Peak

Ski along the wide and nearly level pipeline route to views and near solitude. Except for the horrendous approach up the lower slopes of the Mission Ridge Ski Area, this is an extremely easy tour. First-time skiers would have a wonderful time on the pipeline if they could get there.

As it currently stands, one-ride lift tickets to the start of the tour are no longer available, effectively closing the Pipeline route to beginners. It is hoped that this will change in the near future. In the meantime skiers with good herringbone and snowplow skills will still enjoy this excellent area.

Logging has changed the character of this once avalanche-free tour. The cutting of fire-damaged timber near the western end of the pipeline has created areas of moderate avalanche hazard. Use caution when conditions are unstable.

Access: Drive to Wenatchee and follow the signs to the Mission Ridge Ski Area. Park with the downhill skiers (4,550 feet).

The Tour: Begin your tour by walking behind the lodge to find a groomed, downhill skiers' route which switchbacks up the hill. Ski up along the edge of the groomed road using caution to avoid the banzai beginner downhill skiers. Stay single-file through this section.

Climb the downhill skiers' slope for ½ mile then watch on your right for a

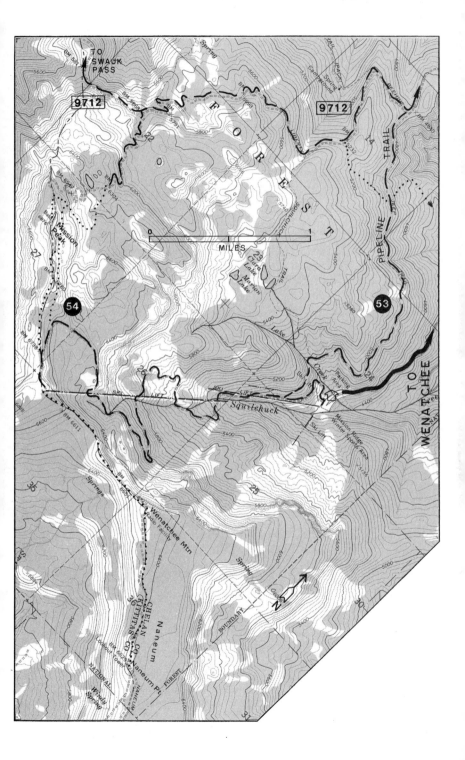

Peek-a-boo view of the Columbia River valley from Pipeline Trail

weathered wooden sign noting the start of the Pipeline Trail. If you join another cat track you have missed the start of the trail by about 75 feet.

The Pipeline Trail heads north, descending about 120 feet in the next 2 miles. Once on the pipeline, the route is obvious and you may settle back to enjoy the tour. Near the 1½-mile mark the Pipeline Trail is crossed by another ski trail marked in blue diamonds. This *most difficult* trail connects Road 7121 with Road 9712.

The Pipeline Trail ends at Liberty–Beehive Road No. 9712. This road is a popular snowmobile route and not very appealing to skiers. However, for those who wish to continue, there is an easy-to-ski trail that starts at the end of the Pipeline Trail, on the other side of Road 9712. This trail follows Spur Road 240 for 1 mile along the crest of a ridge.

Skiers looking for views or a scenic spot for a picnic should climb the steep knoll to the right at the end of the Pipeline Trail. Once up, take a seat on the top of a sandstone pillar and enjoy the view.

54 MISSION RIDGE

Naneum Point

Class: groomed
Rating: most difficult
Round trip: 12 miles
Skiing time: 7 hours
Elevation gain: 2,600 feet
High point: 6,742 feet
Best: January–mid-February
Avalanche potential: none
Map: USGS, Mission Peak

Mission Peak

Class: groomed
Rating: most difficult
Round trip: 12 miles
Skiing time: 7 hours
Elevation gain: 2,700 feet
High point: 6,876 feet
Best: January–February
Avalanche potential: low
Map: USGS, Mission Peak

See map on page 149

A one-ride chairlift ticket used to be the key to two outstanding backcountry tours along the crest of Mission Ridge. In 1995 the ski area suddenly stopped selling one-ride tickets and backcountry skiers were left with no choice but to apply the climbing skins and head up to their old favorite tours as best they can. The climb, through the ski area, adds an extra 4 miles and 2,200-feet elevation gain to both of the tours discussed here, making these once easy trips challenging all-day expeditions.

Once on top you may head east from the chairlift across the rounded ridge crest to views, superb touring, and excellent telemark slopes, ending at the lookout tower on Naneum Point. The second tour heads west from the chairlift to Mission Peak. There are endless views, outstanding telemark slopes, and good touring the entire distance.

Access: Drive to Wenatchee and follow the signs to the Mission Ridge Ski Area (4,550 feet). Check the area map, apply climbing skins, and ski up to the 6,740-foot crest of Mission Ridge.

Naneum Point: From the chairlift terminal at the summit of Mission Ridge, ski left (east) along the ridge crest, following the downhill skiers' trail.

Mount Rainier from the crest of Mission Ridge

The trail soon divides; take either the right or left fork (the right is the easiest) and ski along the ridge to a saddle. Continue east, still following the downhill skiers' tracks.

Ski past the ski-area boundary at ½ mile and climb a long open hill to the radio facility on Wenatchee Mountain (6,742 feet). The view is outstanding; to the southwest is Mount Adams and to the north Glacier Peak and the Columbia River. For telemarking, try the slopes southwest of the peak.

The ridge now turns southeast, descending gradually. Stay to the west of the broad ridge crest to reach the lookout tower 2 miles from the chairlift.

To return to your car, ski back to the chairlift, where you have your pick of the downhill runs. The least difficult heads west from the lift along the ridgecrest and descends 4 miles on a well-graded cat track to the lodge.

Mission Peak: From the chairlift, ski right (west) along the crest of the ridge on a narrow, groomed ski slope. Pass the radio relay station and head down through the trees to a lightly forested basin (6,560 feet). Leave the groomed run here and head left (west) up through the basin, skirting along the base of Mission Ridge. (An alternate method is to ski the rolling ridge crest for 1 mile to the base of Mission Peak.)

Mission Ridge ends at the rock-bound Mission Peak. To reach the summit, ski to the northwest end of the peak and follow the ridge back to the top (6,876 feet). The best skiing is found on the open slopes north of the peak.

To return to your car, ski northeast from the peak, down into a sloping basin following a ski route marked with blue diamonds. At the lower right-hand side of the basin (6,300 feet) ski into the forest on a narrow logging road and continue the descent to Road 9712. Go right (5,868 feet) and ski the road as it winds through two open meadows, climbs for ½ mile, then descends steeply. On the way down you will pass the Clare Lake Trail and several ski trails.

At 6 miles from the chairlift go right on the Pipeline Trail (see Tour 53). Ski south for 2 level miles back to the ski area, where you will turn left to descend back to the parking lot.

MISSION RIDGE

55 MISSION RIDGE TO SWAUK PASS TRAVERSE

Class: multiple use
Rating: more difficult
One way: 28 miles
Skiing time: 2–3 days
Elevation gain: 3,200 feet

High point: 6,720 feet
Best: January–mid-March
Avalanche potential: moderate
Maps: USGS, Mission Peak and
Swauk Pass

Between Mission Ridge and Swauk Pass is a superb traverse of the Wenatchee Mountains. Neither the skiing nor the routefinding on this traverse is difficult, the route being mostly on logging roads packed solid by snowmobile use. The scenery is excellent and there are plenty of opportunities to drop your pack and take a run down open slopes. Campsites may be found along the entire traverse. Plan to melt snow for water.

Access: Leave one car at the Swauk Pass summit Sno-Park on the south side of Highway 97. Then drive north to Highway 2 and follow it east to Wenatchee. Once in town the route to the Mission Ridge Ski Area (4,450 feet) is well signed. Let the parking attendants know you will be leaving your car for several nights. (If there are no attendants, check in at the ski-area or ski-patrol office.)

The Tour: Start your traverse by skiing to Road 9712 via the very scenic Mission Peak Route (Tour 54) or by following easy but much less scenic Pipeline Trail (Tour 53). Mileages are figured for the Mission Peak Route.

Once on Road 9712 the route is straightforward. Go left (northwest) and follow the road along the ridge, sometimes to the right of the crest, sometimes to the left. At 11 miles from the parking lot the road bends south, climbs over a 5,900-foot summit, then divides. The left fork follows a ridge south to Grouse Springs; ignore it.

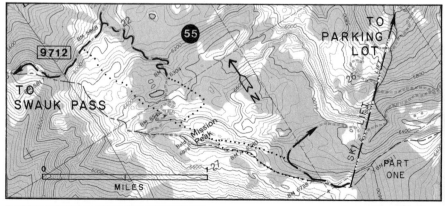

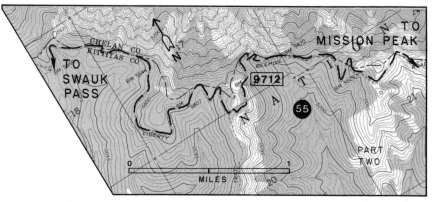

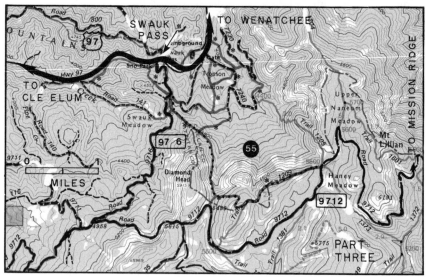

154

Mission Peak

At 13½ miles skirt the edge of steep sandstone cliffs. Do not ski too close to the edge. One mile farther, the road bends south around Mount Lillian. Upper Naneum Meadow is reached at 17½ miles. (A very scenic campsite may be found by going cross-country for 1 mile north of the road at the upper end of the meadow overlooking the Swauk Pass Highway and the Stuart Range.)

At 18 miles the Tronsen Meadow Trail is passed on the right and ¼ mile beyond, also on the right, is the ski trail to Swauk Pass. This trail is well marked with blue diamonds, all intersections are signed, and it reaches the pass in 5 miles. However, the trail is narrow and has several steep sections making it unpleasant when the snow is icy or has a breakable crust. The route also crosses an avalanche chute and is dangerous after a heavy snowfall.

If you choose to continue on Road 9712 you will pass a small wooden cabin on the edge of Haney Meadow at 18½ miles (open to the public and generally occupied in the winter). You then must ski west for 4 level miles to the Table Mountain intersection. Continue straight for 2 more miles, then turn right on Road 9716 and ski north to reach Swauk Pass 28 miles from the start.

LAKE CHELAN

56 STEHEKIN VALLEY TRAILS

Class: *groomed*
Rating: *easiest*
Round trip: *5 miles*
Skiing time: *2 hours–all day*
Elevation gain: *40 feet*

High point: *1,250 feet*
Best: *mid-December–February*
Avalanche potential: *none*
Map: *Green Trails, Stehekin No. 82*

The community of Stehekin lies on a river delta at the head of 50-mile-long Lake Chelan. It is nestled in the forest between two walls of ice-clad mountains and has the appearance of a small Swiss village. Accessible only by boat, Stehekin is the kind of place you read about in books. The community lacks telephones, radios, televisions, supermarkets, and shopping malls.

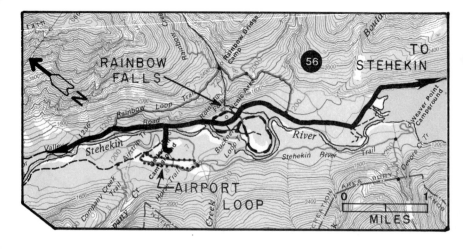

Semi-frozen Rainbow Falls

Everybody knows everybody else. If you enjoy this type of peaceful, yet friendly ambiance, you will find Stehekin a great place to ski.

In 1995, when research was done for this edition, the grooming program was just getting started. Most of the trails in the valley, at that time, were set with tracks for stride and gliding. The only skating lanes were at the Airport Loop and in the orchard portion of the Buckner Loop. Due to the area's location inside the Lake Chelan National Recreation Area, the land is administered by the National Park Service and plans for increasing the

Exquisitely groomed Airport Loop

amount of groomed trails are slow to reach fruition. It will happen, but the date will be determined by the wheels of bureaucracy.

The valley is not an area of endless skiing opportunities; the mountains are too steep and avalanche-prone to be tackled by anyone other than an expert mountaineer skier. However, for skiing at a leisurely pace there are two groomed areas that vie for your attention. This tour describes the valley area close to town. The second area is described in Tour 57.

Access: Just getting to Stehekin is a trip in itself. You may fly from Chelan or ride the *Lady Express* from Chelan or Fields Landing. (See the Introduction for more information about reservations as well as lodging and camping opportunities.) From Stehekin you may walk, hitchhike, or ride the van up-valley to the trails.

The Tour: For challenge and varied scenery, try the Buckner Loop, which begins 3 miles up-valley at Rainbow Falls. After checking out the view of ice-reamed waters at the falls, don your skis and parallel the falls access road back to Stehekin River Road. Cross Stehekin River Road then head out on a groomed trail. At the first intersection go straight. Shortly after cross Buckner Farm Road then cruise along the edge of the Stehekin River to the Orchard where elk and deer are often seen. The loop then parallels Rainbow Creek back to the start. Plans are in the works to turn this loop into a figure-8 which will wind back to the falls.

The Airport Loop is located 4 miles up-valley from the boat dock. Go left at the intersection and cross the Stehekin River. When the road divides again, go left again. In 1995 the Airport Loop was a mile-long, level circuit around the airport runway. The grooming is outstanding, with two lanes for diagonal striding and a skating lane. This is a great area for young skiers, with an almost level track for easy skiing and small hummocks to climb and descend. The scenery is excellent. The Airport Loop will probably be expanded in the future, so keep in touch.

Also in the plans are a 2-mile River Trail and a 7-mile Valley Trail.

57 STEHEKIN RIVER ROAD

High Bridge

Class: groomed
Rating: easiest
Round trip: 5 miles
Skiing time: 3 hours
Elevation gain: 200 feet
High point: 1,620 feet
Best: late December–mid-March
Avalanche potential: none
Map: Green Trails, McGregor
  Mtn. No. 81

Bridge Camp

Class: groomed
Rating: more difficult
Round trip: 16 miles
Skiing time: 7 hours
Elevation gain: 780 feet
High point: 2,200 feet
Best: late December–mid-March
Avalanche potential: moderate
Map: Green Trails, McGregor
  Mtn. No. 81

No winter trip to Stehekin is complete without a tour on Stehekin River Road. There you will see winter at its best: trees trimmed in snow and gleaming with lacy crystals, a roaring river made peaceful by knots of ice and snow, massive icicles streaming off the rocky valley walls, and mounds of fluffy, powder snow.

This winter paradise is caused by long months of sun deprivation. High mountains line both sides of the valley and throughout December and January the sun never rises high enough to reach the valley floor. The result is as beautiful as it is chilly. Dress warmly when you head out to spend a day viewing winter's best.

Stehekin River Road is groomed. In 1995 the skating lane extended to Dolly Varden Camp, a wonderful 8½-mile round trip. Beyond Dolly Varden Camp the road is cut by several avalanche chutes. The bypass trail follows

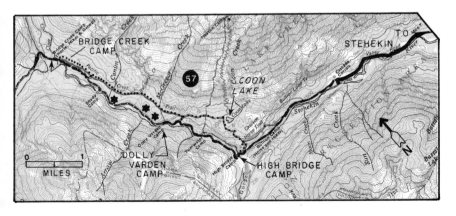

Stehekin River

an old wagon road and is too narrow for grooming, a situation that may change in the future.

Access: The tour begins from the end of the plowed portion of Stehekin River Road. In 1995, the skiing started 8½ miles from the boat dock. You may arrange for a ride to the road-end with the Stehekin Lodge (1,420 feet).

The Tour: From road's end, follow the groomed tracks up-valley through a narrow tunnel of snow-laden trees. The trail leads you across several nearly level terraces left eons ago by the river. Views range from brief glimpses of snow-plastered mountains to occasional looks at the river.

At 2½ miles the road makes its only climb. The ascent ends at the High Bridge Ranger Station (1,620 feet). Just beyond the buildings, the aptly named High Bridge takes the road across the Stehekin River. Deep packed snow hangs over both sides of the bridge: please avoid the temptation of peering over the edge.

Beyond High Bridge, the road heads into a series of switchbacks and begins climbing with gusto. At the second switchback, look right for a short spur road leading to High Bridge Camp which has a three-sided shelter and a pit toilet. Skilled backcountry skiers can join the Pacific Crest Trail here and follow it uphill to Coon Lake or all the way to Bridge Camp. The trail has a variety of markers ranging from orange-painted can lids to official cross-country ski markers.

Views are limited as the road continues up-valley through the forest. The next point of note is a spectacular bridge crossing at 3½ miles, just beyond Tumwater Camp. The snow hangs over the edges, so stay away from the sides of the bridge.

Beyond the bridge the scenery becomes positively dramatic. Icicles hang from rocky cliffs right along the road's edge. Below, the river weaves around large rocks topped with giant bed caps made from snow and ice. Views extend to the towering ridge crests. At 4 miles (1,920 feet) an Old Wagon Road connector trail branches off on the right. Skiers continuing up-valley to Bridge Camp should leave the main road here to avoid the avalanche chutes beyond Dolly Varden Camp which is just ¼ mile ahead. The Old Wagon Road is followed for the next 2¼ miles. At 6¼ miles from the start find a spur trail on the left which leads back to the main road for the final mile-long cruise into Bridge Creek Camp.

LAKE CHELAN
58 ECHO VALLEY

Class: groomed
Rating: most difficult
Round trip: 5 miles
Skiing time: 2 hours
Elevation gain: 400 feet

High point: 3,200 feet
Best: mid-December–February
Avalanche potential: none
Map: USFS, Chelan RD

The Echo Valley Ski Area is patronized by hordes of young kids. Laughing and screaming are the main forms of communication as they zoom up rope tows and zip back down the short, steep slopes. Just beyond this sight of unbridled enthusiasm is a series of elegantly organized cross-country ski trails. Located so near the scene of such high-spirited pandemonium, the silence of the nordic trails is almost deafening.

The Echo Valley Nordic Trails are supported by donations. No Sno-Park permit is required to park or ski. Please leave a donation at the trailhead to help defray the cost of grooming.

Access: From downtown Chelan drive north then west on Highway 150 (North Shore Road) for 4 miles then turn right on Boyd Road. Following the signs to the Echo Valley Ski Area, head up through the hillside residential area and orchards. At 3.4 miles turn right on Boyd Loop Road and after another 1.2 miles go right again on Cooper Gulch Road. At 7.4 miles from Highway 150 you will arrive at the Echo Valley Ski Area. Park at the lower end of the lot (2,800 feet).

The Tour: From the parking lot head out on a wide trail that is groomed for both skating and diagonal striding. This trail is called Silo and is rated *easiest*. Stay left at the junction with the Broadway Trail and glide down-valley for 1 mile to an unmarked intersection near an old wooden silo. Go right and head uphill for about 150 feet to a second junction. Once again stay to the right and continue on uphill (the trail to the left loops back to the silo). After 200 yards is a third intersection. Go left and head out for adventure on Russell's Run. This twisting and winding trail soon leaves the pine forest and heads onto open ridges with expansive views and great peacefulness.

At the end of 1½ miles on Russell's Run you will reach an intersection. Ski left and head up the Screaming Echo Trail which climbs to views at the trip's

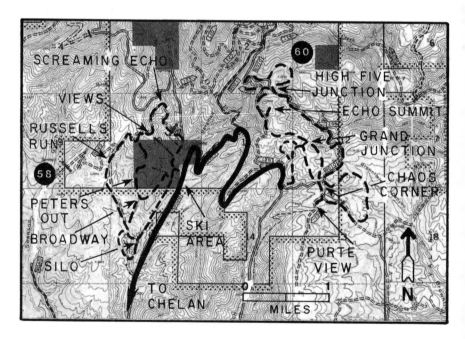

Screaming Echo Trail

3,200-foot high point. Once you have taken in the view you may return to the start in one of three ways: (1) Just beyond the summit are two cat roads. The one on the left is the least rational. This track may or may not be groomed but is guaranteed to raise screams and is rated most difficult or insane. (2) From the summit follow the cat track on the right which is groomed to the top of the ski area. At that point skiers with telemark proclivities will enjoy descending the steep downhillers' slope back to the lodge. (3) The most rational choice is to head back down the Screaming Echo Trail. At the intersection continue down on Peter's Out, a *most difficult* trail which will take you down to the Broadway Trail in 1 mile. Go left on Broadway for the final ½ mile back to the start.

Skiing the Outback

59 THE OUTBACK

Class: *groomed*
Rating: *most difficult*
Round trip: *7½ miles*
Skiing time: *4 hours*
Elevation gain: *1,524 feet*

High point: *4,324 feet*
Best: *mid-December–February*
Avalanche potential: *none*
Map: *USFS, Chelan RD*

To experience the full smorgasbord of skiing opportunities at Echo Ridge (see Tour 60 for more Echo Ridge tours) you must be prepared to break free of the groomed trails and head to The Outback. This rolling adventure to the backcountry is ideal for the skier with an explorer mentality and a pair of skis that love to break trail.

Access: From the center of Chelan head towards Manson on Highway 150 (North Shore Road). After 4 miles go right on Boyd Road. Head up for

3.4 miles then take a right on Boyd Loop Road for 1.2 miles. Go right again on Cooper Gulch Road for 2.8 miles.

The pavement ends at the Echo Valley Ski Resort. Drive past the ski area and the snowmobilers' Sno-Park. Keep your chains handy as the road now narrows and heads steeply up. After 1.4 hair-raising miles you will come to the Zoom Hill parking area (a Sno-Park) located in a turnout at a sharp switchback (2,800 feet).

The Tour: From the parking area walk back down the road 75 feet to find Road 8021, better known as the Zoom Cross-Country Ski Trail, on your right. This road is groomed for diagonal striding and skating. The initial mellow climb provides a short but needed time to warm up. Before long you are climbing with a purpose. Watch out for skiers zooming down.

After climbing for 2 miles, Zoom Road arrives at North Junction where

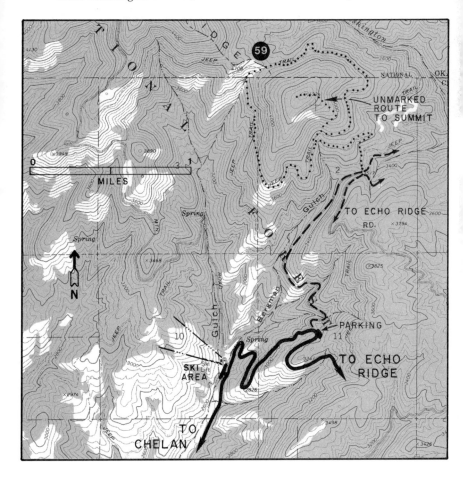

you are faced with a confusing gaggle of snowmobile and ski trails. A large information board, with map, will help you to orient yourself (3,320 feet). From the junction look to your left to find a blue diamond and the "Skier-Only" sign, which mark the entrance to The Outback. At this point you leave the groomed trails and start on the adventure.

The designated route heads northwest from the pass, following an old road ½ mile to a T intersection at 3,520 feet. You may go left or right and circumnavigate the large bald hill in front of you on a series of old roads in 2½ miles. If looking for views and a slope for some turns, ski straight through the T intersection and continue climbing for another ½ mile to the 4,324-foot summit of the hill. Once you have absorbed the view choose the slope with the best snow coverage and see how many turns you can carve. End your day with a quick zoom back to the start.

LAKE CHELAN

60 ECHO RIDGE

Purte View

Class: groomed
Rating: more difficult
Round trip: 4¾ miles
Skiing time: 2 hours
Elevation gain: 150 feet
High point: 3,550 feet
Best: mid-December–February
Avalanche potential: none
Map: USFS, Chelan RD

See map on page 162

Outer Rim Loop

Class: groomed
Rating: more difficult
Round trip: 7 miles
Skiing time: 3 hours
Elevation gain: 625 feet
High point: 3,825 feet
Best: mid-December–February
Avalanche potential: none
Map: USFS, Chelan RD

Echo Ridge Sno-Park is the result of hard work on the part of the Lake Chelan Nordic Club and the Forest Service. This Sno-Park provides skiers with a machine-free area where they can enjoy the excellent scenery of the southern Sawtooth Mountains while experiencing the excitement of skiing on beautifully groomed trails.

For only a moderate investment of energy, the tour to Purte View (say it out loud) is a delightful destination. The Outer Rim Loop tour is a compilation of several loops that take you over and around the entire Echo Ridge area.

Access: From the center of downtown Chelan drive north then west on Highway 150 (North Shore Road) towards the town of Manson. After 4 miles

Skier on aptly named Ridge View Run Trail

go right on Boyd Road following the signs to the Echo Valley Ski Area. After 3.4 miles turn right on Boyd Loop Road and after another 1.2 miles go right again on Cooper Gulch Road. At 7.4 miles from Highway 150 the paved road ends at the downhill ski area. Pass the resort and a snowmobile Sno-Park then continue up on a steep, narrow forest road for 2.6 miles to its end at Echo Ridge Sno-Park (3,400 feet). *Note:* The final 2.6 miles can be very hazardous when icy. Drive cautiously and always carry chains.

Purte View: Begin your tour by skiing up the Chickadee Trail. After an initial steepish climb the trail mellows into an easy traverse. Pass the Upsy Daisy Trail then continue on for 1 mile. At Grand Junction (3,550 feet) go right on the Windsinger Trail and traverse southeast ¾ mile through a young tree plantation to Chaos Corner (3,480 feet). Once again take the trail on the right and glide out on the west arm of the Alley Opp Trail for ½ mile.

At 2¼ miles from the start, find the Purte View Trail (ungroomed) on your right. Head up a low, open hill for ⅛ mile to the crest of a knoll (3,425 feet). From the viewpoint/lunch spot you can look down Purtteman Gulch to Lake Chelan, fog permitting, and on to the Chelan Mountains.

On the return trip, add to your fun by looping back to Chaos Corner on the Alley Opp Trail. This trail has a couple of short, steep descents and at least two rather tight turns, making it very challenging when icy. From Chaos Corner try the ridge-hugging Zippidy Do Da Trail to Grand Junction. Return to the parking lot on the Upsy Daisy Trail.

Outer Rim Loop: Begin your loop by following Chickadee Trail for 1 mile from the parking lot to its end at Grand Junction (3,550 feet). Go left on Ridge View Run and watch for the Stuart Range to the south, the Chelan Mountains to the west, and rolling hills of the Sawtooth to the north. At 1½ miles from the Sno-Park take a short side trip to the crest of 3,825-foot Echo Summit. This ⅛-mile-long trail is not groomed but is easy to ski and the views from the top are outstanding.

Back on Ridge View Run, continue north to reach High Five Junction at 2 miles. Head left on Little Critter Trail, which will return you to High Five Junction at the 3¼-mile point of your loop.

From High Five Junction ski down the Outer Rim Trail. The descent lasts for a mile so zip up your jacket and pull your hat over your ears. Once down, you will spend the next mile in an easy climb to reach Chaos Corner 5¼ miles from the start. At this point you can go left on the Alley Opp Trail, a loop that will add an extra 1½ miles to your day or head back to Grand Junction on Zippidy Do Da. At Grand Junction, go straight for a couple hundred feet then take a right on Upsy Daisy and follow it back to the parking area.

LAKE CHELAN

61 ANTILON LAKES

Class: multiple use
Rating: easiest
Round trip: 3 miles
Skiing time: 2 hours
Elevation gain: 150 feet

High point: 2,300 feet
Best: December–February
Avalanche potential: none
Map: USGS, Manson

A short trip with very little elevation gain makes for lots of fun for young or novice skiers. A campground at the far end of two small lakes provides a good destination.

On weekends this is a moderately popular snowmobile area and skiers should always stay to the right and ski single-file to reduce conflict. Arrange your tour for a weekday and you might have the entire road system to yourself.

Access: From Chelan's city center, follow Highway 150 (North Shore Road) towards the town of Manson. At 6.8 miles, opposite the entrance to

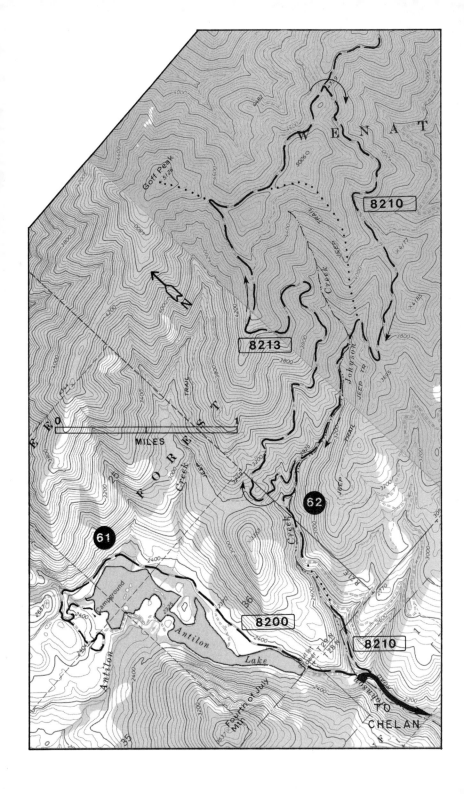

Antilon Lake

Old Mill Park, turn right on Wapato Lake Road. Wind up through apple orchards for 2.4 miles, then turn right on Upper Joe Creek Road, which turns into Road 8200 and arrives at the Sno-Park in 3.9 miles (2,150 feet).

The Tour: Ski up Road 8200, gaining most of the elevation for the tour in an initial short, quick climb. On the left, an earth dam marks the start of the first Antilon Lake. The road contours along the east shore, turning farther east as it rounds the second lake. Above, the hillsides are steep and barren: logged, burned, or both.

As the road begins another climb, note the steep spur road heading down to a clump of trees and campground at the upper end of the second Antilon Lake. If this looks too steep for comfort, continue on about 500 feet to a second access with a more reasonable grade.

Many skiers and even snowmobiles ignore the road, going straight across the lakes and connecting stream. When the ice is solid and covered with an inch or two of new snow, this is great sport. Practice kick-and-glide or skating across the sleek surface. However, be cautious before venturing out onto the ice. If you fall through, you probably won't get out.

If you have a surplus of energy, continue on the road for a short ½ mile beyond the lakes to a saddle on a low ridge. With a little exploration you will find views of Lake Chelan and the Chelan Mountains.

62 GOFF PEAK

Class: *multiple use*
Rating: *most difficult*
Round trip: *10 miles*
Skiing time: *5 hours*
Elevation gain: *2,976 feet*

High point: *5,126 feet*
Best: *December–February*
Avalanche potential: *moderate*
Map: *USFS, Chelan RD*

See map on page 169

Two routes lead to Goff Peak and its magnificent views. One route, rated *most difficult*, follows roads the entire way and may be skied as a loop. The second route is for backcountry skiers whose skills and equipment allow them to leave the roads and head up open slopes where they will find refuge from the whining snowmobiles.

Access: Drive to the Antilon Lakes Sno-Park, elevation 2,150 feet (see Tour 61 for directions).

The Tour: For the road tour, start from the Sno-Park and walk 500 feet back down Forest Road 8200 to Road 8210. Begin skiing north up the groomed snowmobile raceway paralleling Johnson Creek. Fire and logging have left the surrounding hillsides barren, so views commence immediately. Near the end of the first mile reach a major intersection which marks the start of the loop. Go left on Road 8213. (If you are up to a little off-road skiing, leave Road 8210 at the first switchback and continue straight ahead on an abandoned jeep road, eliminating a mile of meandering on the main road.)

Road 8213 climbs steadily, becoming steeper as it nears the ridge crest. Numerous spur roads branch off; however, the main road can generally be identified by its lack of road-number signs. Near the top all

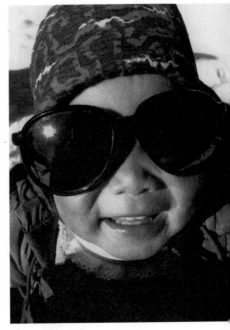

Enthusiastic skier

Summit of Goff Peak

road signs disappear, making the right choice a real guessing game in a snowstorm. Goff Peak is to the north and slightly west of the other hills, so near the summit, veer left and up at all intersections.

The road reaches a narrow saddle at 4,750 feet. Goff Peak is the small hill to the left. Leave the road and ski up to the 5,126-foot summit—the view is outstanding. To the northeast lies Cooper Mountain, one of many points of note on Cooper Ridge. To the west the Chelan Mountains stand out among the Cascade giants. Far below lie miles of orchards along the shores of Lake Chelan.

For the return trip, consider throwing yourself for a loop. From the 4,750-foot saddle, ski south, then east, contouring a full mile to meet Road 8210, the groomed snowmobile route you started the tour on. The descent is obvious and fast.

For backcountry skiers with climbing skins and a yearning to explore, a fun way to approach Goff Peak is up and over the open slopes. From the Sno-Park ski 2½ miles up Road 8210. The road contours then climbs into a broad, open basin with Johnson Creek in the center. Approximately ⅓ mile after crossing the creek leave the road and head uphill following the ridgeline to the summit of the open ridge above. Reach the first summit at 4,185 feet. Continue north-northwest to a small saddle and then contour around the southwest side of a 5,006-foot hill to the logging road in the 4,750-foot saddle below Goff Peak.

63 SMITH CANYON

The Road

Class: multiple use
Rating: easiest
Round trip: 3 miles
Skiing time: 2 hours
Elevation gain: 400 feet
High point: 3,100 feet
Best: mid-December–February
Avalanche potential: low
Map: Green Trails, Twisp No. 84

The Ridge

Class: multiple use
Rating: backcountry
Round trip: 5 miles
Skiing time: 3 hours
Elevation gain: 1,800 feet
High point: 4,200 feet
Best: mid-December–February
Avalanche potential: moderate
Map: Green Trails, Twisp No. 84

No pass or permit is required to enjoy this tour along a quiet Forest Service road. Smith Canyon is tucked away from the mainstream of winter recreation in the Methow Valley and chances are you will have this tour to yourself, even on a weekend. Beginners should stick to the road portion of the tour and leave the bowls and the ridge crest to the backcountry skiers.

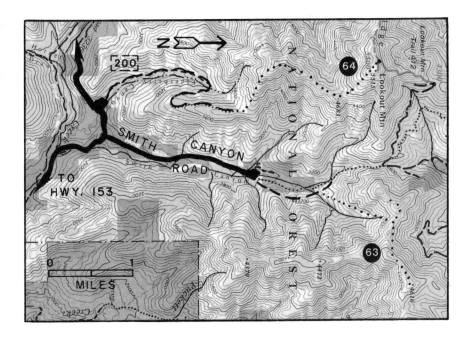

Smith Canyon Road

Access: Drive State Route 153 for 1.2 miles east from the town of Carlton. Turn right on a county road signed "Libby Creek." After 2.4 miles go right on Chicamun Canyon Road. At 3.7 miles from Highway 153, go right again on Smith Canyon Road for 1.9 miles to the end of the plowed road. Park out of the way of other cars and the snow plow (2,700 feet).

The Tour: About 200 feet before the end of the road, find a logging road on the right. Follow the road up through the forest to reach a meadow at 1 mile. Views open up all around. Gaze over a ranch at the edge of the meadow and down Smith Canyon to the Methow Valley. Across the valley the tower on Lookout Mountain is visible.

Continue on the road, losing 200 feet in the next ½ mile. Near the lowest point, where the road crosses a culvert, is the end of "The Road" section of the tour. Backcountry skiers should now leave the road and, heading to the right, climb ¼ mile to a corral. Next, follow a wide trail to the left along the creek bottom as far as possible before switchbacking up steep slopes to the ridge top. (If there is enough snow to cover the rocks and sagebrush, climb directly up the open slopes to a 4,200-foot high point on the ridge.)

Views from the ridge are disappointing. Trees completely cover the north side, so do not expend much energy looking for a window between the branches. Instead, turn around and enjoy the downhill run that makes this trip so worthwhile.

A note about the snow. For off-road skiing in this area you need a couple of feet of snow to cover the small brush and rocks. Snow accumulations of 2 to 3 feet make for excellent skiing. However, accumulations of over 3 feet are unstable on the steeper, open slopes. Years with heavy snowfall are few and far between in the Methow Valley but potentially very dangerous when they occur. If there has been heavy snow buildup, stay off all steeper open slopes (including the slopes of Smith Canyon), skiing only on the ridge tops. If unfamiliar with this area, check for avalanche hazards at the Methow Valley Ranger Station before starting out.

METHOW VALLEY

64 ELDERBERRY CANYON

Class: multiple use
Rating: most difficult
Round trip: 5 miles
Skiing time: 3 hours
Elevation gain: 1,548 feet

High point: 3,900 feet
Best: January–February
Avalanche potential: low
Map: Green Trails, Twisp No. 84

See map on page 173

Elderberry Canyon Road is short and generally ignored by snowmobilers. Their loss is our gain and skiers can enjoy a peaceful tour, even on weekends, in an area where neither Sno-Park nor trail pass is required. Backcountry skiers will also appreciate the access to nearby telemarking slopes.

Note: The road up Elderberry Canyon is quite steep and skiing here can be hazardous when icy.

Access: Drive State Route 153 east of Carlton 1.2 miles then turn onto Libby Creek Road. At 2.4 miles keep right on a road signed "Chicamun Canyon." When the road divides again at 3.7 miles, go left. Continue on another 0.4 mile to Elderberry Canyon Road No. 200. Usually you'll find a small, plowed turnout here for parking (2,362 feet).

The Tour: The road climbs steadily along the forested floor of Elderberry Canyon. The crossing from the west to the east side of the canyon at 1½ miles (3,100 feet) marks the start of assault on the ridge. As the road climbs, the Sawtooth Range pokes over the horizon. Once on the crest you are rewarded

View toward Hoodoo Peak from Elderberry Canyon

with additional views of the Methow Valley, the fire lookout building on Lookout Mountain, and the snow-covered ridges above Smith Canyon. At about 2½ miles, the road ends at the foot of a rounded hill (3,788 feet). Before turning around, ski a little higher on the open slopes to the left for the best views.

In good weather, backcountry skiers can continue on to the top of the open slopes and follow the ups and downs of the ridge crest to Lookout Mountain, approximately 1½ miles farther and 1,700 feet higher.

65 LOUP LOUP—SOUTH SUMMIT

Class: *groomed*
Rating: *easiest–most difficult*
Round trip: *up to 13 miles*
Skiing time: *1–5 hours*
Elevation gain: *up to 709 feet*

High point: *4,659 feet*
Best: *December–February*
Avalanche potential: *none*
Map: *Green Trails, Loup Loup No. 85*

At the summit of Loup Loup Pass are a series of little known, interconnecting, groomed and nongroomed cross-country ski trails. Joined together these trails create a dizzying number of loops. In short, and please excuse the pun, you can loop loop to your heart's content.

The grooming at South Summit Sno-Park is done on an occasional basis on selected trails only. The skiing on these trails is considerably more challenging than on the exquisitely groomed skating trails of the Methow Valley Trail System. Conversely, skiers who came to the Methow with sturdy

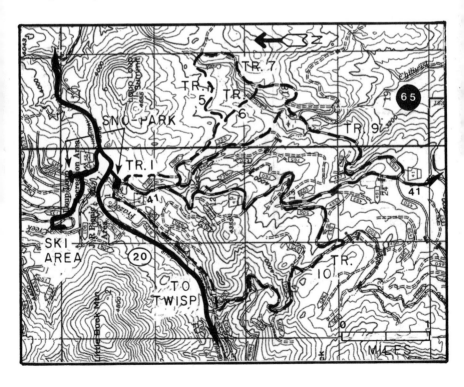

Touring through the forest on Trail No. 5

boots and metal edge skis may find themselves more at home at Loup Loup Pass then down in the valley.

Access: Drive Highway 20 east from Twisp 12.5 miles to the summit of Loup Loup Pass. Turn south on South Summit Sno-Park Road and descend 0.5 mile to the parking area (3,950 feet). If the snowplow has not been by recently you may need to park near the highway and ski into the Sno-Park.

The Tour: No specific loop will be recommended here. All the loops are very enjoyable. Before you head out on your tour, study the information board and map at the south end of the parking area. Choose a loop that looks interesting and matches your skill and energy level then set out with a lunch, a sit pad, and a mind set on adventure.

All the trails are clearly marked with identification number and difficulty rating. Beginner skiers can make an enjoyable loop by combining the No. 1, 7, 5, and 6 Trails. The more adventurous and skilled can make a day of it by looping out on the 7½-mile-long No. 9 Trail. Telemarkers and other thrill seekers can drop a few knee turns on the F Trails that link several loops or cruise around the 5½-mile-long Powerline Trail (No. 10) which has several steep sections.

When you finish one loop, try another one, then another, then another, and another, and another. . . .

66 LOUP LOUP SKI AREA (BEAR MOUNTAIN)

Class: groomed
Rating: easiest–backcountry
Round trip: 20 miles of trails
Skiing time: 2 hours–all day
Elevation gain: 1,370 feet

High point: 5,450 feet
Best: mid-December–mid-March
Avalanche potential: low
Map: Green Trails, Loup Loup No. 85

Virtually unknown to the skiing community of the state of Washington is a gem of an area at Loup Loup Pass. The area, operated by the Loup Loup Ski Resort, has fun intermixed with thrills and spills for all skiers. This is a place where your skis are appropriate (be they narrow skating skis or metal-edged telemark specials). Diagonal striders with traditionally narrow skis will find the beautifully groomed tracks diversified enough to be fun for children and beginners, as well as for experts. Casual tourers, gliding along on their wider skis, will find the friendly atmosphere and views to be exhilarating. Backcountry and telemark skiers with their heavy boots, metal

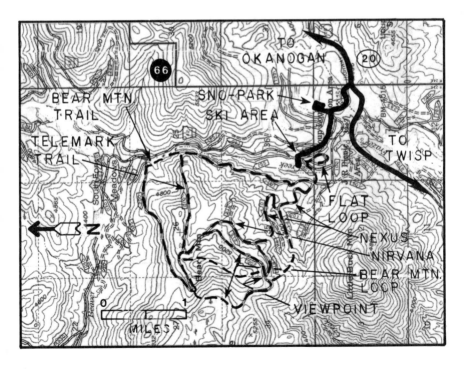

179

Checking out the view from Nexus Trail

edges, and reduced cambers have groomed trails that are designed with them in mind, with steep slopes for carving turns.

The Loup Loup Ski Area trails are operated on a fee basis. This fee is incredibly minimal when compared to charges in the valley. Fees are collected when the ski area is operating or when someone is at the office. Grooming occurs only on days of operation, which are Saturday, Sunday, and Wednesday. A Sno-Park permit is not required.

Access: From the intersection of Highways 153 and 20, located just east of Twisp, drive east on Highway 20 to the summit of Loup Loup Pass. At the summit take the first left. Pass the North Summit Sno-Park then continue on 1.2 miles to the ski area (4,080 feet). If the ski area is not operating, there will be a closed gate 0.2 mile up the road. A small area is plowed for parking. Do not block the gate.

The Tour: Beginners can get the feel of their skis by trying out the Flat Loop located just south of the ski lifts. This loop, actually a figure-8 with an optional shortcut, is 3 miles long and runs through meadows and forest. The youngest skiers may also enjoy the 1½-mile Short Loop, which has just enough of a slope to excite the age 6 and under crowd. Both of these trails are rated *easiest*.

If you are looking for scenery, try the Nexus Trail, which climbs to views on Bear Mountain. After climbing steadily for a mile the trail reaches the Viewpoint (4,800 feet). You then have a choice of trails; Nexus, Nirvana, or the Bear Mountain Loop. If the Bear Mountain Loop is chosen you may traverse around the rolling summit then follow Nirvana back to Nexus for a 5-mile tour. Of course you can easily expand the tour by skiing down the Bear Mountain Trail to the Eclipse Trail (4,400 feet). At this point you may follow either the Eclipse Trail (most difficult) or Road 42 (groomed for snow-mobiles). The Eclipse Trail ends after a long ¾ mile at the Telemark Trail where you will be faced with a short but extremely challenging descent to the Gabion Trail. Most days, the ¾-mile-long road cruise with the snow-mobiles is the lesser of the two evils. The Gabion Trail ends at the parking lot. This extended loop is about 7 miles long.

Telemark is the only trail that actually crosses over the crest of 5,450-foot Bear Mountain. This challenging trail is a wide, hard-packed swath that heads straight up to the rolling summit then descends in a similar fashion. If you stay on the hard-packed trail you will need climbing skins to ascend and controlled linked telemarks to descend. You may prefer to do most of your climbing either on the Nexus or the Bear Mountain Trail. On the descent you may cut wider turns on the lightly forested slopes next to the trail rather than in the narrow track.

METHOW VALLEY

67 BUCK MOUNTAIN LOOKOUT

Class: *multiple use*
Rating: *most difficult*
Round trip: *9 miles*
Skiing time: *5 hours*
Elevation gain: *2,675 feet*

High point: *6,135 feet*
Best: *January–March*
Avalanche potential: *moderate*
Map: *Green Trails, Loup Loup No. 85*

Buck Mountain Lookout is one of the best tours to the backcountry in the Methow area. After a winter storm the snow will put a grin on your face. The spring skiing here, after the sun has thawed the corn, is equally delightful. The telemarking is so much fun you may care less about the views, which, incidentally, are excellent.

Buck Mountain Lookout

Note: Parking may be a problem. If a space has not been plowed out, come back some other day.

Access: Drive to the summit of Loup Loup Pass then proceed down the east side 2.5 miles and find a road on the left signed "Buck Mountain Road." Look carefully for the sign: in midwinter it is nearly covered with snow (3,460 feet). Parking is limited with space for four cars if everyone packs together or two small cars if not.

The Tour: In its first mile Buck Mountain Road passes several well-signed intersections, first with Powerline Road followed by Summit Creek Road. Later intersections are not so well signed. To add to the confusion, Buck Mountain Road is on state land, where the road numbering is a bit haphazard. The road starts as B100, changes to OM B1000,

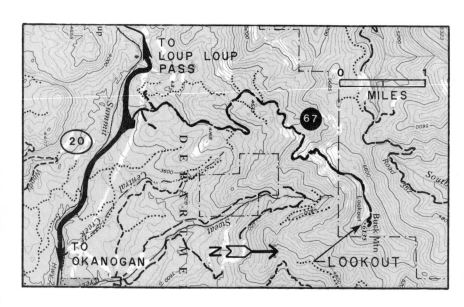

Buck Mountain Road

and eventually has no number at all. Carry a good topographical map, and consult it when in doubt.

After 1½ miles of steady climbing, the ascent eases off on a broad bench and Central Creek Road joins on the left (4,120 feet). Buck Mountain Road switchbacks up to a narrow saddle, then levels off again, contouring northeast for a mile into an open basin.

At 3 miles you'll reach an unmarked intersection (4,900 feet). Stay right and climb to an open ridge. The route is now obvious because the lookout is visible. The road is frequently covered by snowdrifts, so simply stay to the east side of the ridge until directly below the lookout. Here the narrow road leads straight up to the summit with its 360-degree views.

68 SUN MOUNTAIN

Class: *groomed*
Rating: *easiest–most difficult*
Round trip: *nearly 37 miles of trails*
Skiing time: *3 hours–all day*
Elevation gain: *1,387 feet*

High point: *3,987 feet*
Best: *January–February*
Avalanche potential: *low*
Map: *MVSTA, Sun Mountain*

Sun Mountain Lodge is perched 1,000 feet above the Methow Valley and is at the center of a network of groomed cross-country trails that lead to scenic overlooks, mountain passes, and lakes. Whether novice or veteran, skaters and diagonal striders will appreciate the diversity of the skiing opportunities as well as the excellent scenery. Most trails at Sun Mountain are groomed for skating as well as diagonal striding.

Access: From Twisp, drive Highway 20 north 5.3 miles. Turn left on Twin Lake Road for 1.8 miles, then go left on Patterson Lake Road for 5.6 more miles to Sun Mountain Lodge. Stop by the ski shop for a map, equipment rentals, trails information, and a ski pass (required for all trail users). Parking at the lodge itself is for guests, but 0.6 mile below the lodge is a Day-Use parking area located just off Thompson Ridge Road (2,700 feet). A Sno-Park permit is not required.

The Tour: The Day-Use area is a delightful starting point. At the parking lot are outhouses and a warming hut. On weekends a wood stove heats the hut and food and warm drinks may be purchased.

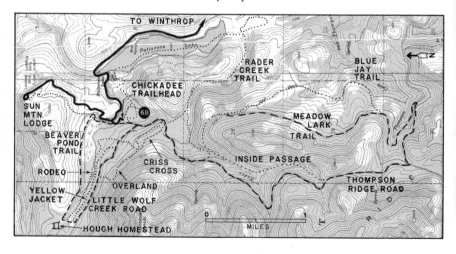

Skier near Sun Mountain Lodge

185

Most trails are groomed for skating

If this is your first visit, start your explorations by heading up from the parking area to Thompson Ridge Road. Go right and descend to the Beaver Pond Trail then follow it through aspens to the old Hough Homestead and shelter. For your return try the roly-poly Yellowjacket Trail or the well-graded Little Wolf Creek Road.

For scenery as well as exercise, Thompson Ridge Road is a sure bet. Stay with the groomed road 4 miles to a major intersection (3,480 feet) with the Meadow Lark Trail. Follow Meadow Lark to Blue Jay. The Blue Jay Trail winds through the forest, passing several scenic overlooks before it returns you, 2 miles later, back to the Meadow Lark Trail. Continue on the Meadow Lark Trail until it meets Upper Inside Passage and ends. At this point you may either return to Thompson Ridge Road or add a few thrills to your tour with a warp-speed descent down the *most difficult* Inside Passage, which rejoins Thompson Ridge Road ½ mile above the Day-Use area.

Adventure seekers should make a loop down to Patterson Lake. From the Day-Use parking area, ski up Thompson Ridge Road ½ mile then go left on Lower Inside Passage. After a short distance you will arrive at a three-way intersection. Go left for an exhilarating descent down Rader Creek. At the bottom go left again and follow the trail across Patterson Lake (check at the Sun Mountain ski shop for the condition of the ice before you start). At the far end of the lake go left again and follow the Patterson Resort Trail uphill to Chickadee. At this point either a left or a right will take you back to the start. The loop is 5 miles long and has a *most difficult* rating.

Blue Buck Road

69 BLUE BUCK MOUNTAIN

Class: *multiple use*
Rating: *more difficult*
Round trip: *4 miles to Cougar Lake,*
   10 miles to road-end
Skiing time: *2–4 hours*
Elevation gain: *1,200 feet to lake,*
   3,400 feet to road-end

High point: *5,400 feet*
Best: *mid-December–mid-March*
Avalanche potential: *low*
Map: *Green Trails, Twisp No. 84*

Neither an expensive trail pass nor an expensive Sno-Park permit is required to ski this tour and, in the Methow Valley, that is truly unusual. However, and more importantly, this tour through the Methow Valley Wildlife Recreation Area is a scenic masterpiece with views over the valley to the glacier-clad heartland of the North Cascades. Of course, because no fee is charged to ski here, you are likely to find yourself all alone and you may

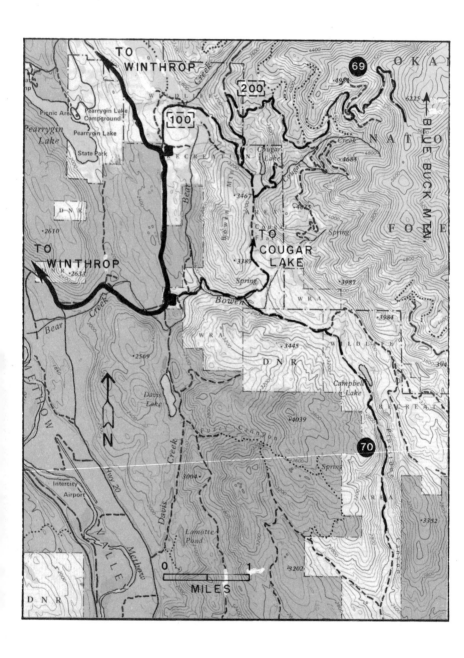

even have to break your own trail. The Methow Valley Wildlife Recreation Area is closed to motors from October 1 to December 31 while the deer are migrating from the high mountains to their wintering grounds along the Columbia River. The rest of the winter you may have to share the road with a snowmobile or two.

Access: From the center of Winthrop follow the main street north. As it bends and heads uphill it becomes Bluff Street. After 1.6 miles go right on Pearrygin Road. Head up until the road levels off at 5.3 miles then watch for Road 100 on the left. Park out of the way of local traffic (2,000 feet).

The Tour: Views begin almost immediately as you ski up Road 100. Pass two side roads to the left and two to the right before arriving at the first switchback and an intersection at 1½ miles (3,120 feet). To reach Cougar Lake go right for ¼ mile then left for ⅛ mile (3,200 feet). For more views, stay left at 1½ miles and continue the climb. Follow the road as it ascends gradually for another ½ mile to an intersection. Go right on Road 200 to the National Forest Boundary (3,400 feet). From here, numerous side roads diverge but, provided the signs are not buried, there should be little trouble following the main road. In another mile there is a four-way junction—go straight through onto Road 225. At 5 miles from the plowed road (5,400 feet), the road ends. Trees make it impractical for all but backcountry skiers to continue to the top of Blue Buck Mountain, but the descent back down the road is exhilarating.

View of the North Cascades and Methow Valley from Blue Buck Road

70 PIPESTONE CANYON

Class: *multiple use*
Rating: *most difficult*
Round trip: *10 miles*
Skiing time: *5 hours*
Elevation gain: *750 feet*

High point: *2,900 feet*
Best: *January–February*
Avalanche potential: *low*
Map: *Green Trails, Twisp No. 84*

See map on page 188

Not far above the town of Winthrop an exotically beautiful canyon lies hidden amongst the open, rolling hills. Its steep walls have been carved by wind and water into the intriguing rock formations that give the canyon its name. Best of all, the location of this canyon in the heart of a wildlife preserve guarantees that it can be traveled only by those with four legs or two skis.

Skier on Lester Road

Skiing in this area requires neither a Sno-Park permit nor a ski trail pass. Snowmobiles are rare except on weekends.

Access: Coming into the south end of Winthrop on Highway 20, drive across the Methow River bridge and take an immediate right on Twisp–Winthrop Eastside Road. In 0.2 mile go left on Center Street and then, in a few yards, right on Castle Avenue. Drive south 1.6 miles and turn left on Bear Creek Road. Head uphill 1.8 miles to the pavement's end. Park in a small plowed area on the right side of the road (2,150 feet).

The Tour: Ski up Lester Road. The climb is steady and even steep in sections. The two spur roads passed on the left lead north around Bowen Mountain to Cougar Lake. At 3½ miles the road enters a broad meadow (2,900 feet). Once you are in the meadow leave the road and ski to the right. You may have to hunt around a bit to find the windswept road to Campbell Lake. The way descends, passing the lake to reach the entrance to Pipestone Canyon. Continue on the road, descending the canyon ½ mile to the pipestone formation. If time allows, ski the entire 2-mile length of the canyon, losing only 480 feet. Rounded hills at the lower end offer good skiing. The quiet visitor may see deer or coyotes.

METHOW VALLEY

71 RENDEVOUS PASS HUT TO HUT

Class: groomed
Rating: more difficult
Round trip: 10 miles
Skiing time: 1–4 days
Elevation gain: 1,450 feet

High point: 3,985 feet
Best: mid-December–February
Avalanche potential: none
Maps: Green Trails, Doe Mtn. No. 52
and Mazama No. 51

Anyone who has ever spent a long winter night in a tent will immediately recognize the appeal of hut-to-hut skiing. Just north of Winthrop, in the Rendevous area, are five interconnected huts to take the sting out of winter camping.

Besides the huts, the Rendevous area offers excellent touring and skating on groomed trails, as well as backcountry exploring and outstanding slopes for telemarking.

The Rendevous Pass area is part of the Methow Valley Ski Touring Association trail system and a pass must be purchased, available in Twisp and Winthrop, before skiing the trails. Reservations and hut information can be obtained by calling Rendezvous Outfitters, Inc. at 1-800-422-3048. Gear hauling services are also available.

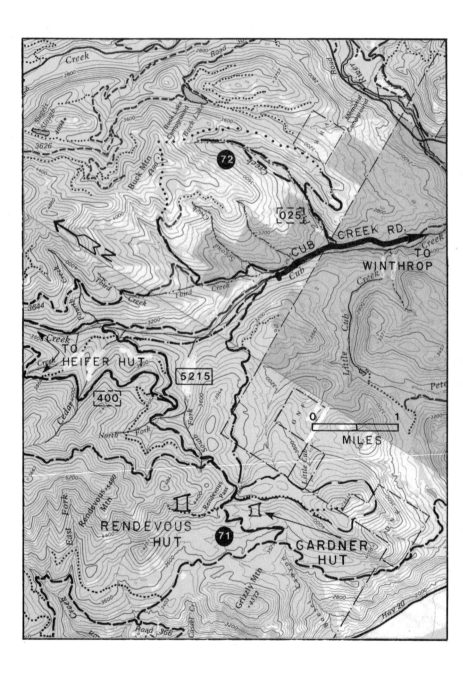

Zipping down a groomed ski trail below Rendevous Pass

Tours to Rendevous Pass start near Mazama at the Goat Creek Sno-Park (Tour 77) or from the east at Cub Creek. The Cub Creek access is the shortest and the best for day trips.

Access: Drive Highway 20 west 0.1 mile from Winthrop. Turn right on West Chewuch River Road and follow it for 6.6 miles. At Cub Creek Road turn left for the final 2.1 miles to the end of the plowed road. Go right up a narrow lane for the final ascent to the parking area (2,635 feet).

The Tour: Ski up Cub Creek Road (now called Road 52). After ¼ mile, the road divides. Follow the left fork ⅛ mile down to Cub Creek, then take the first road on the left and cross the creek. Ski up this road 300 feet to another fork and go right on the Heifer Hut Trail (the left fork is the Little Cub Creek Trail, one of two possible return routes).

The route heads up-valley through alternating forest and meadow for 2 miles. Except for two steep climbs, the trail is nearly level until it meets the Cow Creek Trail. Turn left here and ski uphill into the South Fork Cow Creek Valley.

Four miles from the start, Spur Road 400 branches off on the right. This road is part of the Cedar Creek Loop, which leads to Banker Pass and the Heifer Hut (the second of the two alternate return routes). Continue on up the Cow Creek Trail. Pass the upper end of the Little Cub Creek Trail at 5 miles. After another 200 feet, the Cougar Mountain Loop Trail takes off on the left—continue straight.

Rendevous Pass is reached at 5½ miles (3,985 feet). The pass area is in trees. For views east and west ski to the left a few hundred feet up a small knoll. To reach Rendevous Hut, ski over the pass about 300 feet then follow the trail markers to the right (off the road) through the forest for ½ mile.

For those staying at the hut, there are miles of marked trails to explore such as the 4-mile groomed track around Cougar Mountain, a 13-mile ungroomed round trip to Fawn Peak, or a long descent to the Methow River Valley past Gardner Hut, Cassal Hut, and Fawn Hut.

The return may be made by Little Cub Creek or Cedar Creek. The trip back by Little Cub Creek is on a steep 4½-mile trail that is difficult when icy. The Cedar Creek Loop is for the energetic. It is a meandering 10-mile ski from the pass to the parking area. The trail is not steep and the views of Buck Mountain make this an excellent tour for long-distance skiers.

METHOW VALLEY

72 BUCK MOUNTAIN LOOP

Class: multiple use
Rating: backcountry
Round trip: 10 miles
Skiing time: 7 hours
Elevation gain: 1,900 feet

High point: 4,490 feet
Best: mid-December–mid-March
Avalanche potential: low
Map: Green Trails, Doe Mtn. No. 52

See map on page 192

Buck Mountain is a perfect example of all things that have made the Methow Valley famous among free-heeled skiers—open slopes for telemarking, peaceful countryside for backcountry touring, and vistas of the North Cascades and the Pasayten Mountains. The loop route up and over Buck Mountain is not groomed. Be prepared to break trail. In 1995 neither Sno-Park permit nor trail pass was required to ski here.

Access: Drive to the Cub Creek skiers' parking area as described in Tour 71.

Open slopes near summit of Buck Mountain

The Tour: Walk back down the road 0.3 mile. Just below First Creek look to your left (north) to find the start of Road 025. After crossing a cattle guard, the road climbs steeply up a narrow valley. At ¾ mile (2,900 feet), the road splits. Go right, climbing gently as you round the ridge to reach road's end at 2 miles. Traverse to the ridge top, bypassing the first hump, then continue north, keeping a little to the right (east) of the ridge crest. At 3,700 feet leave the ridge crest and traverse around the west side of a major knoll. After ¼ mile begin climbing again and head to the crest of the summit ridge. Once on top go left to reach the top of Buck Mountain at 5 miles (4,490 feet). The views extend far and wide. The Chewuch River valley, Paul Mountain, and Cougar Mountain are only a few of the sights. On a clear day the impressive peaks of Gardner, Midnight, and Oval are visible.

The downward route chosen will depend on the skier's ability. Begin by descending southwest to meet a Forest Service road at 3,680 feet. Ski on down, staying left at all intersections to reach the groomed Cub Creek Trail at 8 miles. Go straight for a final ¼ mile back to the start.

To challenge your telemarking skills, ski from the top of Buck Mountain directly to the parking area. Follow the Forest Service road down about ¼ mile until a stock-loading ramp and corral are visible far below. Head down to this corral, dropping 1,160 feet in almost nonstop turning. If you plan right you make your last telemark just before you reach your car.

Heifer Hut

73 HEIFER HUT

Class: *groomed*
Rating: *more difficult*
Round trip: *10 miles*
Skiing time: *5 hours*
Elevation gain: *1,365 feet*

High point: *4,000 feet*
Best: *mid-December–mid-March*
Avalanche potential: *none*
Map: *MVSTA, Rendevous*

Heifer Hut is one of six winter getaways in the Rendevous Hut system. The hut is reached by a peaceful ski tour through open pine and spruce forest. Once you reach the hut you are treated to a delightful tree-framed view of Buck Mountain.

If you don't happen to be lucky enough to be making an overnight stay, the hut is still a great destination for a day trip. Hut courtesy requires that you do not enter the hut if another party is already inside. If you light up the wood stove, please leave a donation for the wood.

The well-signed trail to the hut is groomed for diagonal striding and skating. An MVSTA trail pass is required; however, a Sno-Park permit is not necessary to park at the trailhead. For hut information and reservations contact Rendezvous Outfitters, Inc. at 1-800-422-3048.

Access: Drive to the Cub Creek skiers' parking area (see Tour 71).

The Tour: From the parking area, ski across the field to intersect Cub Creek Road then head up-valley ¼ mile. When the road divides, follow the groomed trail to the left. Immediately after crossing Cub Creek, the trail divides. Go right, following the signs to Heifer Hut and the Cow Creek Trail. (The left fork is the groomed Little Cub Creek Trail to Rendevous Pass.)

The ascent is generally gradual as you glide through forest and clearcuts. However, a couple of short descents serve to keep you alert and two very steep climbs will certainly help to keep you warm. At 3 miles the Heifer Hut Trail meets the Cow Creek Trail (3,200 feet). Stay right. After another ¼ mile you will ski past a sheep loading ramp. At this point the trail makes a sharp bend and begins to climb steeply and steadily. Watch out for descending skiers who are having so much fun that they either cannot or do not want to stop. The next junction is reached at 4¼ miles (3,900 feet). To the left is the Cedar Creek Loop, an alternate return route. For now stay right on the nearly level trail that meanders into the Heifer Creek drainage, crosses the creek, then wanders back out again. At 4¾ miles you will encounter the steepest climb of the tour. This final ¼-mile push to the 4,000-foot hut is breathtaking.

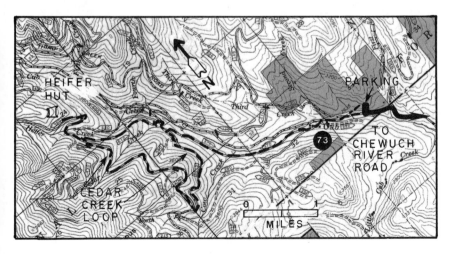

74 BUCK LAKE

Class: multiple use
Rating: most difficult
Round trip: 6 miles
Skiing time: 3 hours
Elevation gain: 1,080 feet

High point: 3,200 feet
Best: mid-December–February
Avalanche potential: low
Map: Green Trails, Doe Mtn. No. 52

Buck Lake lies on a wide bench below Buck Mountain, west of Doe Mountain, east of Fawn Peak, north of Blue Buck Mountain, and not far northwest of yet another Buck Mountain. Despite the overworked name, Buck Lake makes a delightful destination for a short day tour.

Access: Drive to Winthrop on Highway 20. When the highway makes a 90-degree turn in the center of town, leave the main road and continue straight north between the rows of western-style buildings. Before long the road bends uphill then heads up the Chewuch River valley. After 6.8 miles cross the Chewuch River. Go right on West Chewuch River Road, which soon

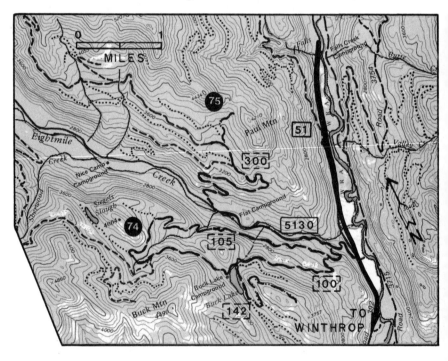

Fence near Buck Lake Campground

turns into Forest Road 51. Continue upriver another 2.5 miles to Eightmile Sno-Park (2,120 feet), located just opposite Eightmile River Road No. 5130.

The Tour: Eightmile River Road is a groomed snowmobile route. Luckily, throughout the week and on most weekends few machines use it and skiing is quite pleasant. The road immediately starts to climb, making a couple of switchbacks before reaching the Buck Lake turnoff in a short mile (2,360 feet).

Go left on Buck Lake Road No. 100 and continue the steep climb which promises a fast descent on the return trip. At 1½ miles pass a semi-abandoned logging road on the right and continue to climb. Around 2 miles the road straightens and traverses northwest through logging cuts. Across the valley you'll see the rocky walls of Paul Mountain.

At mile 3, the road divides again. The left fork leads to a boat ramp at the south end of Buck Lake then on up Spur Road 142 to the summit of a low hill overlooking the lake. The right fork heads to the campground. If more exercise is desired, 4 extra miles may be added to the tour by skiing rarely used logging roads in a long loop. Starting from Buck Lake, ski to the right, past the campground, for 1½ miles. The first time the road divides stay right on Road 100. The next time it divides, go right on Road 105. Stay on this road as it loops east, then bends south, returning to Buck Lake Road 1½ miles from the Sno-Park. Few views or snowmobiles bless or curse this loop.

METHOW VALLEY

75 FLAT CAMPGROUND AND PAUL MOUNTAIN

Class: *multiple use*
Rating: *more difficult*
Round trip: *4 miles to Flat Campground*
Skiing time: *2 hours*
Elevation gain: *440 feet*

High point: *2,560 feet*
Best: *January–mid-March*
Avalanche potential: *moderate*
Map: *Green Trails, Doe Mtn. No. 52*

See map on page 198

High in its valley, Eightmile Creek flows calmly, almost lazily, below snowcapped mountains. Snow bridges span the creek along its meandering course. As the lazily descending creek approaches the end of the valley its character changes. Hidden fury is unleashed and the creek gushes, bubbles, and carves its way down to the Chewuch River valley. This tour follows the picturesque Eightmile Creek from the Chewuch River, up along the turbulent gorge to red-barked ponderosa forests and peaceful snow-covered meadows in the quiet valley above. Skiing this area is a must for the complete Methow Valley experience and well worth the noise and inconvenience inherent in touring a groomed snowmobile route.

Access: Drive to the Eightmile Creek Sno-Park (2,120 feet) (see Tour 74).

The Tour: Eightmile River Road is located opposite the Sno-Park and begins climbing immediately through the forest. At the end of the first mile, pass the Buck Lake Junction. The road then levels off and carves its way across precipitous walls above Eightmile Creek. Near 2 miles, a shallow dip leads to a crossing of Eightmile Creek followed by a gentle climb. Stay on the left (creek) side of the road here. The bank on the right drops surprisingly large snow sloughs onto the road on wet or warm days.

Shortly beyond the bridge is Flat Campground, well named to be sure. This makes an excellent turnaround point for a short tour. For more exercise and views, ski on up-valley to the second road on the right (located about 500 feet beyond the campground). Head uphill on Spur Road 300, which climbs steadily over the flanks of Lamb Butte towards Eightmile Ridge. The best views occur after 2 miles when you look down on Eightmile Creek and across to Buck Mountain.

Paul Mountain

76 METHOW VALLEY VIEW

Class: *multiple use*
Rating: *easiest*
Round trip: *5 miles*
Skiing time: *3 hours*
Elevation gain: *700 feet in, 200 feet out*

High point: *3,300 feet*
Best: *January–February*
Avalanche potential: *low*
Map: *Green Trails, Mazama No. 51*

A bird's-eye view of the Methow Valley and a great backdoor entrance to the popular skier-only trails of the Grizzly Mountain–Rendevous Pass area highlight this tour.

This route is not a part of the MVSTA so no trail pass is required to ski here, nor is a Sno-Park permit required for parking. What a bargain. However, the

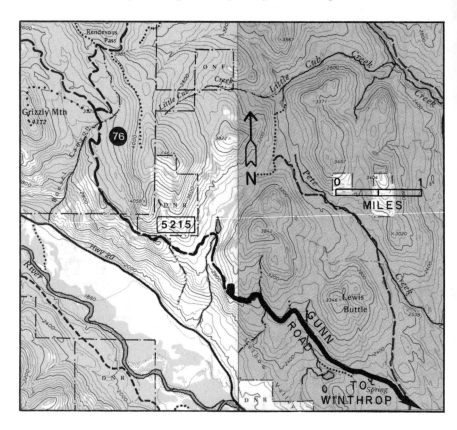

Farms below Lewis Butte

road is plowed on a low-priority basis and reaching the start of the tour may be difficult after a heavy snow fall.

Access: Drive west from Winthrop for 0.1 mile on Highway 20, then turn right on West Chewuch River Road for 1 mile. At Rendezvous Road, also called County Road No. 1223, go left and head up 1 mile to a fork. Turn left on Gunn Road for 3.4 miles to the end of the plowing. Usually you'll find a turnout just big enough to park one or two cars (2,800 feet).

The Tour: Beyond the parking spot the county road makes a horseshoe bend as it circles a farm field, rounds a bend in the hillside, goes up a short, steep pitch, and enters the forest. At 1 mile skirt along the brink of a steep cliff with an aerial view of the Methow River 1,000 feet below. The valley is only half the view; across the way Gardner Mountain heads a long line of North Cascades summits. From the viewpoint the route enters the woods. Half a mile farther, you will reach the National Forest boundary where the county road becomes Forest Road 5215. At 2½ miles your road intersects the groomed Fawn Creek–Rendevous Pass ski trails near Grizzly Mountain. To ski the 1¾ miles to Rendevous Pass on Road 5215 you need a trail pass.

If you are backcountry equipped and wish to ski farther without a pass, head up the untracked slopes of Grizzly Mountain. The most popular approach heads around the base of the mountain and ascends the north ridge to the 4,372-foot summit. After fresh snowfall the descent is a classic.

METHOW VALLEY

77 FAWN HUT AND BEYOND

Class: groomed
Rating: most difficult
Round trip: 7½ miles
Skiing time: 4 hours
Elevation gain: 1,380 feet

High point: 3,460 feet
Best: December–February
Avalanche potential: moderate
Map: Green Trails, Mazama No. 51

It's like a little piece of Norway with open mountain views, mountain huts, and well-groomed trails. Unlike Norway, the area is maintained by the Methow Valley Ski Touring Association and you must have a pass to ski here. Hut reservations and information can be obtained by calling Rendezvous Outfitters, Inc. at 1-800-422-3048. Gear hauling service to the hut is available.

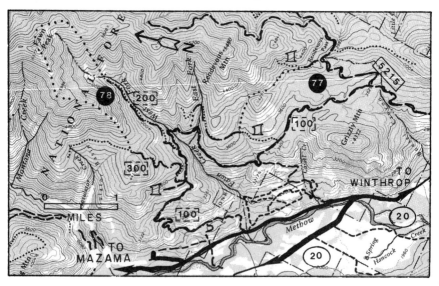

Fawn Creek Trail near Fawn Hut

Access: Drive west of Winthrop 8.5 miles on Highway 20. Just before crossing the Methow River, turn right on Goat Creek Road and head toward Mazama. After 3.4 miles turn right again on Goat Creek Forest Road No. 52 and follow it for 0.4 mile to the Sno-Park (2,080 feet). Parking here requires a Sno-Park permit. If you do not have a permit you may use the Day-Use lot at the entrance of Mazama Country Inn. Let the Inn staff know you will be leaving your car for several days. Parking at the Inn means you will be skiing an extra 3 miles just to reach Fawn Hut.

The Tour: From the south end of the Goat Creek Sno-Park follow the groomed ski track on a winding and rolling course through the forest. After 20 yards pass a junction with the trail from Mazama Country Inn. Continue straight ahead for ¼ mile to reach a second intersection. Go left on the Lower Fawn Creek Trail for a steep climb up the forested hillside.

At ¾ mile from the Sno-Park the Lower Fawn Creek Trail joins a wide logging road and broadens to include two sets of tracks for diagonal striding as well as a wide skating lane (2,400 feet). For the next 2½ miles the trail climbs relentlessly, gaining elevation with a couple of long switchbacks. Views expand at every corner.

At 3¾ miles from the parking lot a groomed spur road branches off to the left heading uphill to Fawn Hut (3,460 feet), where you will be rewarded with a delightful view of Gardner Mountain to the west and Rendevous Mountain to the south. Day skiers are welcome to enter the huts as long as no other group is already in residence. If you do use the hut please leave it clean, and if you light a fire leave a donation to cover the cost of the wood.

If you are not stopping at Fawn Hut, continue straight ahead for an easy glide into the Fawn Creek drainage on the Upper Fawn Creek Trail. The trail remains nearly level for the next 2 miles then, gradually, dips to the West Fork Fawn Creek drainage. Once over the creek the trail begins an easy descent into Rendevous Basin. At 2½ miles from Fawn Hut the Upper Fawn Creek Trail ends. Continue on the Rendevous Basin Trail for a gradual climb through the gentle basin between Rendevous and Grizzly Mountains. In this section you will twice intersect the Cassal Creek Trail which loops out from the Cassal Hut. Rendevous Pass (3,985 feet), reached at 6¾ miles from Fawn Hut, is buried in trees but, by following the signs to the hut (⅛ mile northwest), you'll snag views of Gardner Mountain and the surrounding countryside.

78 FAWN PEAK

Class: *groomed*
Rating: *backcountry*
Round trip: *13 miles*
Skiing time: *8 hours*
Elevation gain: *4,497 feet*

High point: *6,577 feet*
Best: *January–mid-March*
Avalanche potential: *low*
Map: *Green Trails, Mazama No. 51*

See map on page 204

Ask a group of skiers which peak offers the best view in Washington and there will be a heated debate and no consensus. We expect the jury to be out for a long time on this one because the competition is incredibly tough. However, even if Fawn Peak does not have the best view in Washington, it is incontestable that the 360-degree panorama from the summit is a masterpiece.

Four approaches offer access to the peak: the Southwest Rib Route, the West Fork Fawn Creek Basin Route, the Southwest Rib Backcountry Route, and the High Route from Rendevous Pass. The first three approaches can be skied in a long day. The approach from Rendevous Pass is a two-day affair.

Access: Drive to the Goat Creek Sno-Park (2,080 feet) (see Tour 77).

The Southwest Rib Route: From the south side of the Sno-Park, follow directions given in Tour 77 and ski the well-marked trail 3¾ miles to the Fawn Hut junction (3,460 feet). At this point the Southwest Rib Route leaves

View of Methow River valley and North Cascades from Fawn Peak

the groomed trails. Look up the hill for the unmarked, but regularly skied Spur Road 300. Follow this ungroomed road on a steadily uphill climb. At ¾ mile avoid a tempting spur road to the right.

Continue on Spur Road 300 to a 4,180-foot saddle then leave the road and head up and to the north along the crest of the ridge. The first chance to mark progress is a 5,986-foot rounded knoll about ¾ mile from the summit. From the knoll, follow the ridge for a short descent and then a final push to the summit (6,577 feet).

Oh! What a view. It simply does not end. The peaks of the Pasayten, rounded in summer, are massive under their coats of snow. The high North Cascades are dominated by Gardner, Silver Star, Tower Mountain, and Azurite Peak. Finally, the Methow Valley and Okanogan Mountains unfold at your feet.

To descend, backcountry ski down through Insulator Basin and return directly to the parking area or head down through West Fawn Creek Basin.

West Fork Fawn Creek Basin Route: From the Goat Creek Sno-Park follow the groomed trails for 3¾ miles to the Fawn Hut junction (see Tour 77). Continue straight on the groomed Upper Fawn Creek Trail. At ½ mile past the Fawn Hut junction go left on Spur Road 200. This ungroomed road parallels West Fork Fawn Creek while climbing steeply. At 4,600 feet, enter a basin where the road ends. Cross the first of two small creeks and immediately start climbing through the planted rows of trees to the steep open slopes above. The destination is the ridge crest (5,780 feet). Once on the ridge ski left, northwest, to the summit of Fawn Peak.

Southwest Rib Backcountry Route: For this approach you will need a good map and a pair of climbing skins. From the Goat Creek Sno-Park head south for a few feet then begin climbing. Follow the rambling line of the ridge to the summit of Fawn Peak. No trail pass is needed to ski this route.

High Route from Rendevous Pass: Following the directions in Tour 71 ski to Rendevous Pass. Head north following the ridge crest over a series of peaks including 5,480-foot Rendevous Mountain. Stay on the ridge and you'll reach Fawn Peak 5 miles from the pass, a great day trip from the hut.

METHOW VALLEY

79 GOAT MOUNTAIN ROAD

Class: *multiple use*
Rating: *more difficult*
Round trip: *3–14 miles*
Skiing time: *1–6 hours*
Elevation gain: *240–2,640 feet*

High point: *up to 4,800 feet*
Best: *mid-December–March*
Avalanche potential: *low*
Map: *Green Trails, Mazama No. 51*

Just because your three-day pass has expired is no reason to leave the Methow Valley. If you have a Sno-Park permit you have all that is required for an outstanding tour. You may even start to wonder why you wasted so much time skiing on the valley floor.

Goat Mountain Road is part of an extensive groomed snowmobile trail system. Expect some mechanical competition on weekends and holidays. On weekdays you may have the entire road system to yourself.

Access: The tour begins at the Goat Creek Sno-Park, elevation 2,080 feet (see Tour 77).

The Tour: From the Goat Creek Sno-Park follow Road 52 north. Skiing is easy, especially if the groomer has been by recently. The climb starts gradually, allowing plenty of time to warm up. A short descent at ½ mile leads to a crossing of Goat Creek which is followed by an easy, mile-long climb to an excellent viewpoint located at the first switchback (2,420 feet), the first of the many turnaround points. Beyond the viewpoint the rate of climb increases as Road 52 heads up Goat Creek valley to reach a major intersection, and the second good turnaround spot, at the 2-mile point (2,800 feet). Go left on Goat Mountain Road No. 5225 and begin a steady climb up the forested hillside. If this seems like a lot of work just think how fun the descent will be. After a

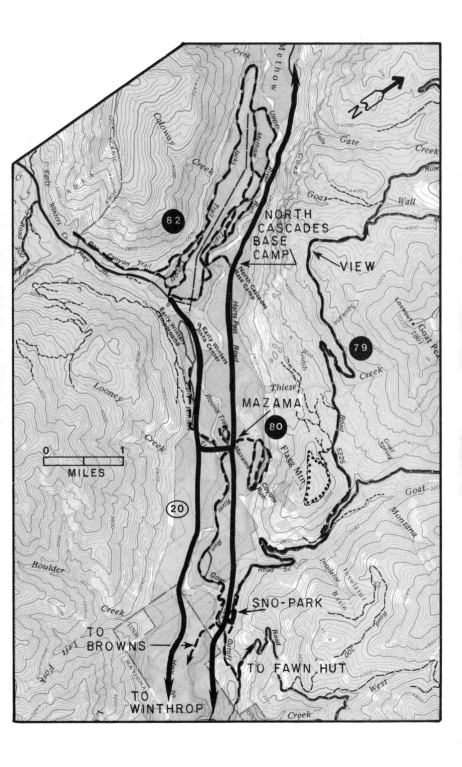

NORTH
CASCADES
BASE
CAMP

VIEW

82

79

MAZAMA
80

0   1
MILES

20

SNO-PARK

TO
BROWNS

TO FAWN HUT

TO
WINTHROP

Spectacular North Cascades scenery from Goat Mountain Road

mile of climbing the road levels briefly (3,400 feet). Note Spur Road 050 on the left. This road may be followed to the 4,004-foot crest of Flagg Mountain, another excellent destination and turnaround point.

Road 5225 continues its steady ascent, soon rewarding your efforts with views across the valley to Driveway Butte. Views continue to expand to include Sun Mountain, Sandy Butte, and a host of glaciated North Cascades summits. Before long the road switchbacks and at 6 miles, shortly after passing Spokane Gulch, you will pass another excellent viewpoint and turnaround spot. At 7 miles (4,800 feet) a sharp bend to the northeast marks a final turnaround point for day trips.

80 MAZAMA

Class: groomed
Rating: more difficult
Round trip: 7 miles
Skiing time: 3 hours
Elevation gain: 200 feet

High point: 2,150 feet
Best: late December–mid-February
Avalanche potential: none
Map: MVSTA, Mazama

See map on page 209

Diagonal striders or the even more aerobic skaters will find plenty of room to roam on immaculately groomed trails in the Mazama area of the Methow Valley. Your route for this tour winds along the terraces overlooking the snow-covered riverbed of the Methow River then heads into the forest for a change of pace. The final leg of the loop is a cruise through open fields along the base of the Goat Wall.

As with most tours in the Methow Valley Trail System, you can lengthen or shorten your trip by choosing a slightly different route through the intertwining network of looping trails. A Sno-Park permit is not needed for this tour; however, you must have an MVSTA trail pass.

Access: From Winthrop, drive west on Highway 20 for 14.6 miles. At Lost River Road go right and head across the valley to a four-way intersection. Go straight through the intersection to the Mazama Country Inn access road. A few feet beyond the intersection look for the Day-Use parking area on the right (2,150 feet). Ski rentals and accessories are available at the inn.

The Tour: From the Day-Use parking carry your skis back to the four-way intersection then cross the road. Start your loop on the Lower River Run Trail located on the left (south) side of Lost River Road.

For the next 2 miles your skis will take you through small meadows along the river's edge. At the end of the River Run Trail stay left on Post Loop Road which heads across Goat Creek and over a plowed road to reach the Goat Creek Cutoff Trail at 2¾ miles. Leave Post Loop Road here and go left for the hardest climb on the loop. When icy this ascent is murderous and best walked. Once up, the trail crosses Goat Creek Road to intersect the Lower Fawn Creek Trail. Go left and head back up-valley.

Ski through the forest on a trail that rolls with the terrain. At 3¾ miles the trail divides again. Following the signs to Mazama Country Inn, stay left. The trail crosses the Goat Creek Sno-Park access road then heads into several short but steep descents before crossing Goat Creek on a sturdy bridge.

At 4¾ miles the trail leaves the forest and heads across level fields. Before

Groomed trail through open fields at Mazama

long the trail divides again; go right following the scenic portion of the Goat Creek Loop Trail. When the two legs of the Goat Creek Loop rejoin, go straight ahead on the Inn Run Loop Trail for ¾ mile then take a right and, shortly after, a second right to reach the Coyote Run Trail for a short hill-climbing adventure and a view. At 6¼ miles stay to the right on Goat Wall Loop and complete your tour with a scenic cruise along the base of the Goat Wall. Walk the Inn access road back to the Day-Use parking area to return to your car at 7 miles.

81 METHOW VALLEY COMMUNITY TRAIL

Class: groomed
Rating: easiest–more difficult
One way: 16 miles
Skiing time: 1 hour–3 days
Elevation gain: 400 feet

High point: 2,110 feet
Best: late December–February
Avalanche potential: none
Map: MVSTA, Rendevous

Spanning the length of the valley from Mazama to Winthrop, the Methow Valley Community (MVC) Trail joins the major ski areas together making it the pièce de résistance of the entire MVSTA trail system.

You do not need to ski the entire distance in one day. The MVC Trail is designed to be skied in comfortable day trips starting and ending at convenient parking points. Groups with two cars can arrange one-way adventures. The most exotic and delightfully decadent method is to ski from inn to inn.

In the description that follows, the trail has been divided into three sections. If these sections seem too long, don't worry—you will have fun even if you ski only half the distance.

Mazama Country Inn to Brown's Bed and Breakfast: This section of the trail is 5 miles long (10 miles round trip) and is rated *easiest*. Following the directions in Tour 81 drive to Mazama and park in the Day-Use area. Walk back from the parking area and cross the road to find the Lower River Run on the left. When the Lower River Run ends at 2 miles, continue on Post Loop Road. At 2¾ miles pass the Goat Creek Cutoff. Views remain limited until the trail zips across the snow-covered bed of the Methow River on the

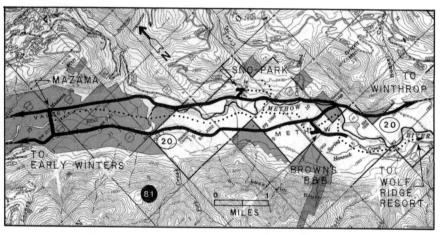

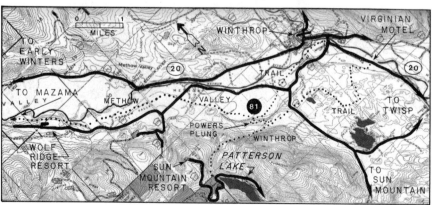

Parts of the MVC Trail have an urban flavor

Tawlks-Foster suspension bridge at 3½ miles. The final section of this tour is a cruise through open fields. Just before reaching Brown's at 5 miles, the trail crosses Highway 20.

Brown's Bed and Breakfast to Wolf Ridge Resort: This very enjoyable 5-mile section of the trail (10 miles round trip) is rated *more difficult*. Along the way you will ski past farms, fields, and houses while meandering through forest and meadows along the edge of the Methow River. At Wolf Ridge Resort you are welcome to make use of their lovely warming hut where you can eat your sack lunch or buy something to warm up in the microwave. You may also buy a self-service hot drink to sip by the wood stove before you head back. To reach the start of the tour, drive west from Winthrop on Highway 20 for 9.1 miles. At Wolf Creek Road, go left for 0.1 mile. The Day-Use parking area is located on the right.

Wolf Ridge Resort to Winthrop: This very scenic 6-mile, *easiest* section of trail (12 miles round trip) is the best area for beginning skaters and diagonal striders near the town of Winthrop. To reach the trailhead at Wolf Ridge Resort, turn left on Twin Lakes Road just before Highway 20 crosses the Methow River to enter Winthrop. After 1.3 miles turn right on Wolf

Creek Road and follow it for 4.4 miles to the resort entrance.

From the resort, ski south on the Edwards Outback Trail through fields and pastures. The trail climbs to a higher terrace then crosses Wolf Creek Road. (Limited parking is available, 2.5 miles from Twin Lakes Road, if you want to shorten your trip.)

At 3¼ miles is a major intersection. To the right, the Power's Plunge Trail heads up into the hills towards the Winthrop Trail, Sun Mountain Resort, and the Virginian Motel. The MVC Trail continues straight ahead on its level and scenic course through the fields. At 5 miles the trail recrosses Wolf Creek Road. After 6 miles the trail ends at the Spring Creek Ranch Bed and Breakfast parking area (located 0.1 mile up Twin Lakes Road from Highway 20).

Skiers near Wolf Ridge Resort

METHOW VALLEY

82 EARLY WINTERS

Class: groomed
Rating: easiest–more difficult
Round trip: 10¾ miles of trails
Skiing time: 5 hours
Elevation gain: 600 feet

High point: 2,800 feet
Best: late December–February
Avalanche potential: none
Maps: MVSTA, Mazama, and Green Trails, Mazama No. 51

See map on page 209

Great scenery, old ranch houses, numerous looping trails, easy rolling terrain, and a warming hut make this a great area for skiers young, old, and in-between.

Early Winters is part of the MVSTA and you'll need a trail pass to ski here. Parking is free. *Note:* Some of the trails in this area cross private land. Please behave accordingly.

Access: From Winthrop, drive west 16.6 miles on Highway 20 to the end of the open road at Early Winters Campground (2,240 feet). You may also access these trails from the North Cascades Base Camp reached by driving 14.4 miles west from Winthrop then turning right on Lost River Road. Cross the valley to Mazama then go left. After 2.2 miles go left on the Base Camp road. Park in the Day-Use area.

The Tour: Numerous possibilities await: short loops or long loops, take your pick. For a short loop try skiing the River Run/Methow Trail Loop. This loop is only 5¼ miles long and incorporates the best of the area. The easiest access is from North Cascades Base Camp. Descend from the parking area to cross the Methow River then go right and climb to an intersection of the River Run and Methow Trails. Go straight and ski up-valley on the Methow Trail. Glide or skate past old farms with dramatic views of ice-coated Goat Wall, returning to your starting point on the River Run Trail. If you get cold, take a rest stop at the small warming hut.

For a longer loop combine Methow Trail and Jack's Trail. These two trails form a nearly level, 6½-mile loop around the Early Winters area which is ideal for beginning skaters. The parking area at Early Winters Campground provides the most convenient access for this loop.

If you would like to do a bit of climbing followed, of course, by a descent, try the Doe Canyon Trail. This is a *more difficult* trip. A well-used bench marks the top of the climb. The run back is fast and fun as long as you have a good grasp of the basic principles of stopping. Early Winters Campground is also the most convenient access point for this tour.

Warming hut at Early Winters

83 CUTTHROAT CREEK

Class: self-propelled
Rating: backcountry
Round trip: 11 miles
Skiing time: 7 hours
Elevation gain: 2,300 feet

High point: 6,800 feet
Best: April–mid-June
Avalanche potential: moderate
Map: Green Trails, Washington Pass
No. 50

The first and last ski run of the season can be taken on the sheltered slopes below Cutthroat Peak. The North Cascades Highway is closed by avalanches for most of the winter so time your visit for right after it reopens in the spring.

Access: Drive the North Cascades Highway (State Route 20) either 4.7 miles east from Washington Pass or 10.8 miles west from Early Winters Campground. Turn off the main highway at Cutthroat Creek Road for the final 1 mile to the Cutthroat Trailhead (4,500 feet).

The Tour: The lower portion of the trail may be snow-free, so be prepared to carry the skis for the first mile. From the horse ramp, head up-valley for several hundred feet before crossing Cutthroat Creek on a substantial bridge. On the north side of the creek the trail makes a gentle switchback, then bee-lines up-valley.

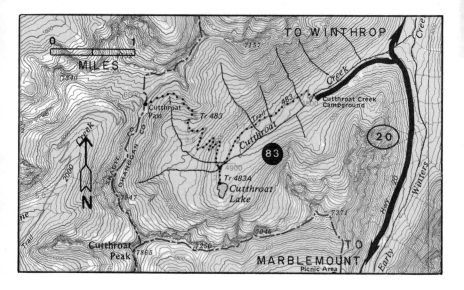

Porcupine Creek Basin

In a wooded area at 1¾ miles the trail forks (4,900 feet). The left-hand fork continues on ¼ mile to Cutthroat Lake. The right-hand fork, Trail 483, heads up toward Cutthroat Pass and the ski slopes. If you should lose track of the trail under the snow on the way up, just continue straight up the steep hillside.

About 1½ miles above the Cutthroat Lake junction the trail enters the meadows. Avoid the rocky spurs on the ridge crest and switchback northwest to reach the rounded Cutthroat Pass at 6,800 feet. Bowls on either side of the pass provide excellent skiing. On the west side of the pass, ski across the Pacific Crest Trail and descend the upper reaches of Porcupine Creek Basin before heading back up.

SUGGESTED READING

AVALANCHE SAFETY

Fraser, Colin. *Avalanches and Snow Safety.* New York: Charles Scribner's Sons, 1978.

Graydon, Don, ed. *Mountaineering: The Freedom of the Hills,* 5th ed. Seattle: The Mountaineers, 1992.

LaChappelle, E. R. *ABC of Avalanche Safety,* 2d ed. Seattle: The Mountaineers, 1985.

ENJOYING THE OUTDOORS (PROPER CLOTHING, SKI EQUIPMENT, WINTER CAMPING)

Brady, Michael. *Cross-Country Ski Gear,* 2d ed. Seattle: The Mountaineers, 1988.

Tejada-Flores, Lito. *Backcountry Skiing.* San Francisco: Sierra Club Books, 1981.

Watters, Ron. *Ski Camping.* Pocatello: The Great Rift Press, 1989.

HOW-TO

Barnett, Steve. *Cross-Country Downhill,* 2d ed. Seattle: Pacific Search Press, 1979.

Bein, Vic. *Mountain Skiing.* Seattle: The Mountaineers, 1982.

Gilette, Ned, and John Dostal. *Cross-Country Skiing,* 3d ed. Seattle: The Mountaineers, 1988.

FIRST AID

Carline, Jan, Martha Lentz, and Steven Macdonald. *Mountaineering First Aid,* 4th ed. Seattle: The Mountaineers, 1996.

Wilkerson, James A., M.D., ed. *Medicine for Mountaineering,* 4th ed. Seattle: The Mountaineers, 1992.

INDEX

ABOUT THE AUTHORS

Vicky Spring and Tom Kirkendall are experienced outdoor people. The couple travels the hills in summer as hikers, backpackers, and mountain bikers; when the snow falls, they grab their cross-country skis and keep on exploring. They studied at the Brooks Institute of Photography in Santa Barbara, California, and are now building their careers together as outdoor photographers and guidebook authors.

Tom and Vicky have written numerous outdoor titles for The Mountaineers. Vicky is the author of *Glacier National Park and Waterton Lakes National Park: a Complete Recreation Guide*, *Cross-Country Ski Tours of Washington's South Cascades*, *100 Hikes in California's Central Sierra and Coast Range*, and *Bicycling the Pacific Coast*. Tom is author/photographer of *Mountain Bike Adventures in Washington's South Cascades and Olympics* and *Mountain Bike Adventures in Washington's North Cascades and Puget Sound*.

So many trails, so little time.

THE MOUNTAINEERS, founded in 1906, is a nonprofit outdoor activity and conservation club, whose mission is "to explore, study, preserve, and enjoy the natural beauty of the outdoors. . . . " Based in Seattle, Washington, the club is now the third-largest such organization in the United States, with 15,000 members and five branches throughout Washington State.

The Mountaineers sponsors both classes and year-round outdoor activities in the Pacific Northwest, which include hiking, mountain climbing, ski-touring, snowshoeing, bicycling, camping, kayaking and canoeing, nature study, sailing, and adventure travel. The club's conservation division supports environmental causes through educational activities, sponsoring legislation, and presenting informational programs. All club activities are led by skilled, experienced volunteers, who are dedicated to promoting safe and responsible enjoyment and preservation of the outdoors.

If you would like to participate in these organized outdoor activities or the club's programs, consider a membership in The Mountaineers. For information and an application, write or call The Mountaineers, Club Headquarters, 300 Third Avenue West, Seattle, Washington 98119; (206) 284-6310.

The Mountaineers Books, an active, nonprofit publishing program of the club, produces guidebooks, instructional texts, historical works, natural history guides, and works on environmental conservation. All books produced by The Mountaineers are aimed at fulfilling the club's mission.

Send or call for our catalog of more than 300 outdoor titles:

 The Mountaineers Books
1001 SW Klickitat Way, Suite 201
Seattle, WA 98134
1-800-553-4453: e-mail; Mbooks@mountaineers.org